)TTERY

GAYLORD MG

FRONT COVER: Black and red stylized bird motifs adorn a yellow jar by Rachel Nampeyo from Polacca (1951).
BACK COVER: Poolisie of Sichomovi decorated a yellow jar with another variation of a black and red stylized bird design (1933).

CONTEMPORARY
HOPI POTTERY

by Laura Graves Allen

Museum of Northern Arizona
Flagstaff, Arizona

Contemporary Hopi Pottery was published by the Museum of Northern Arizona with the help of funding from the National Endowment for the Arts.

CONTENTS

Foreword vii

Preface ix

Acknowledgments xi

Hopi Pottery: The Historic Period 13

Color Portfolio 48

The Hopi Craftsman Exhibition 67

Afterword 91

Photo Captions 93

Catalog 101

Hallmarks 125

Bibliography 126

FOREWORD

The Museum of Northern Arizona first opened its doors in the old Flagstaff Woman's Club in August 1928. Within six months Lyndon L. Hargrave became the first archaeologist of the new institution. Almost immediately he went to the Hopi Villages as a member of the National Geographic Society Beam Expedition under the direction of dendrochronologist Dr. A. E. Douglass to look for old timbers used in constuction. Hopi houses grow outward and upward from a core of perhaps one or two rooms where the oldest ceiling beams are located and which are used for storage because they have little or no light. As Hargrave visited the various pueblos, he noticed old pottery storage jars and bowls of various sizes tucked away in corners of these storerooms. Upon inquiry he found that they had been made by mothers and grandmothers of the owners who considered them of little value. He suggested to Dr. Colton, Director of the Museum, that it would be desirable to purchase as many of these pieces as could be found to form the basis of a Hopi pottery collection. Dr. Colton agreed.

Hargrave's collection of 41 pieces of Hopi ceramic art, dating back to the 1860s, was the very first collection of Hopi enthnologic specimens the Museum made. Beginning with the First Hopi Craftsman Exhibition at the Museum in 1930, new pieces were added almost every year up to the present so that now more than a century of Hopi pottery is represented. Students and scholars have studied it over the years, but relatively few people are aware of its exsistence.

At long last an illustrated catalog of Hopi pottery in the Museum of Northern Arizona is being published, through the valiant efforts of Marsha Gallagher, Robert Breunig and last, but certainly deserving the most credit, Laura Graves Allen, upon whom the responsiblity of finishing the study was inevitably thrust. It gives me great satisfaction to see this catalog in print, for it is something I should have undertaken many years ago when I was Curator of Anthropology at the Museum. Probably it is just as well I did not. Knowledge of pottery history has greatly increased in the past few years, and this study is of much greater value than it would be if it had been written twenty years ago.

KATHARINE BARTLETT

PREFACE

The Museum of Northern Arizona sits on one of the largest natural laboratories in the Southwest. Its location was chosen for this reason by the museum's founders Mary-Russell Ferrell Colton and Harold Sellers Colton. The Coltons' deep interest in the continuity of cultures from prehistoric to contemporary times prompted them to pioneer a variety of research topics that are still current today.

Their fascination with and love for the Hopi people and their culture—prehistoric, historic, and contemporary—was expressed in many ways. One manifestation of this is the Hopi ethnographic collection at the museum. There were other, perhaps equally important expressions: the first, and still unsurpassed, guide to kachina doll identification (Colton 1949) was one important result of Dr. Colton's interest. Mary-Russell Ferrell Colton's appreciation for Hopi basketry led to her work on Hopi dyes (Colton 1965), a work that remains a basic reference tool. Her interest in Hopi jewelry led ultimately to the development of the Hopi Silvercraft Cooperative Guild.

The Coltons supplemented all of these activities with avid collecting—selecting representative items for the museum's permanent collections. Their work established the museum as the repository for the most extensively documented contemporary Hopi ethnographic collections in the United States.

ACKNOWLEDGMENTS

This publication has been the work of a number of people. Initial funding was secured from the National Endowment for the Arts through two proposals authored by Marsha Gallagher, now at the Joslyn Art Museum. Robert Breunig, Chief Curator at the Heard Museum, added his particular flavor to the project and through his linguistic approach to the utilitarian pieces reopened research questions pondered by the Coltons and Katharine Bartlett.

A number of curatorial assistants spent countless hours updating catalog entries and assisting in the monumental documentary projects of this work. To those I owe my thanks. A debt of gratitude is owed Kimberly Huber, Cindy Knox, Deborah House, and Robert A. Coody. Katharine Bartlett and E. Charles Adams answered my questions, listened to my thoughts, and were more help than they know.

However, all of our work pales in comparison to those ladies who make the pots. There are no words capable of expressing my appreciation of those who, like Rena Kavena, year after year turn over some of their best pieces for our show; who, like their mothers and aunts before, capture the essence of timelessness in their pots and share that spirit with all of us.

There are no experiences to equal sitting in Garnet Pavatea's kitchen listening to her describe the huge pots her mother made and hoping that her attempted duplications don't explode in the firing, or watching Susanna Denet pick out a piece from all of the collection and saying "my mother made this." This is the vitality, the continuity of spirit, of Hopi pottery. This is the work of all those who have come before.

Glimpses of Hopi village life show the use of storage jars. Kopta Collection

HOPI POTTERY
THE HISTORIC PERIOD

The Hopi people have lived in the American Southwest for at least two thousand years. Their abandoned villages and farmlands cover the northeastern corner of Arizona, and new sites and other evidence of the continuity of their culture are still being uncovered.

About six hundred years ago, for reasons not totally understood, Hopi populations began moving into the present area. Pueblo villages with apartmentlike configurations and open air plazas were established on three distinct fingers of land protruding from the southern end of Black Mesa. On the westernmost mesa, Third Mesa, the village of Oraibi was established by A.D. 1100. Other villages, abandoned by 1690, dotted the area on both First and Second Mesas. Walpi and Hano on First Mesa were established by 1700; Sichomovi by 1750. Shungopovi, Mishongnovi, and Shipaulovi were also established by the eighteenth century on Second Mesa. In the last one hundred years the following villages have been established: Keams Canyon, a governmental/trading center east of First Mesa; Polacca, a trading center at the foot of First Mesa; Kyakotsmovi, Hopi Tribal Headquarters location and a trading center at the eastern foot of Third Mesa; Hotevilla and Bakabi on Third Mesa; and Moencopi near Tuba City to the west.

Traditional Hopi material culture has its roots buried deeply in the prehistoric past. The techniques and technologies of basketry, textile, and pottery production have remained constant throughout time. Raw materials changed only with the movement of people and with changes in the environment. The production and function of decorated and undecorated baskets and trays; straps, bags, ropes, clothes, ceremonial costumes, and wearing blankets; and decorated and undecorated storage jars, cooking pots, and dippers have remained constant throughout time.

Extensive archaeological research conducted during the last one hundred years in and near the Hopi villages shows a continuing pattern. The continuity of Hopi culture manifests itself in a number of ways, but the humble potsherd is the element appearing most often. It is also most effective in reflecting subtle culture change. These durable pieces speak volumes to the archaeologist and have helped establish the cultural chronology of the Southwest. Numerous books and articles have been written about prehistoric ceramics (Colton 1953, 1954, Colton and Hargrave 1937), and the reader is urged to turn to those studies.

Dr. and Mrs. Colton, Clay Lockett, and David Breternitz judge pots for a Hopi Craftsman Exhibition.

Ceramic production in the Hopi region reflects a twelve-hundred-year-old tradition. Any time demarcation or classification is, of necessity, arbitrary and artificial. However, for the purposes of this short overview, we have tried to establish an appropriate time frame reflecting Hopi history, Hopi ceramic production, and the focus of this book: the contemporary Hopi pottery collection at the Museum of Northern Arizona.

In addition to pottery, the museum has well-documented collections in basketry, kachina dolls, jewelry, and textiles. Each of these crafts, though not treated in this work, has had an important role in the development of contemporary Hopi material culture.

The contemporary Hopi ceramic collection is composed of 1,053 pieces representing over one hundred years of production. Over half (58%) of these pieces were purchased by the Coltons and the museum staff—either through direct contact with the makers or through the museum's annual Hopi Craftsman Exhibition. The remainder of the collection represents donations from the private sector. Because well over half of the collection was obtained by museum personnel, the composition of the collection represents a conscious effort to document the evolution of contemporary Hopi pottery and to show representative samples of what was produced. As a result, the entire collection is well documented and represents an invaluable resource to both scholars and laymen.

To date, the collection has been the focus of a number of studies (Sikorski 1968, Love 1973, and Stanislawski, Stanislawski and Hitchcock 1976). However, with the exception of this publication, no definitive study of the complete range of contemporary Hopi ceramics has been attempted. This study will trace the evolution of contemporary Hopi pottery from its historic roots and identify some of the external forces that have effected its

change. It is hoped that this work will stimulate more interest in Hopi ceramics, from both the non-Hopi consumer and the Hopi potter-producer.

The development of Hopi pottery parallels historical events affecting the Hopi people. Fearing reprisals following the Pueblo Revolt of 1680, many Rio Grande Pueblo groups moved west to stay with their Hopi relatives. The Tewa, one of the groups, were given a village location on First Mesa and farmlands in return for the protection they offered to the Hopi.

The Rio Grande people brought with them an equally old and sophisticated pottery tradition. Their works, melding the native aesthetic with new Spanish design elements, had a profound effect on the Hopi pottery produced at the time. The Hopi ceramics produced at the beginning of the eighteenth century reflect this influx of new people and ideas. Hopi pottery designs show strong eastern Pueblo influence, especially from Zia and Zuni. Layout is similar to pottery made by the Keres and Acoma peoples and is characterized by stacked panels, split feathers, vertical and diagonal scallops, running diamond, and s-shaped frets terminating in straight wing or terraced elements. Sharp-tipped feathers, terraced elements, split/solid triangles, and fringed aprons also are common (Adams 1979:28). Bowl interiors are painted with a central bottom panel design. Rims are always red, and on jars the red slip may extend into the interior. Jars have a high, pronounced shoulder and concave bottoms; the design panel is limited to the area above the shoulder.

By the end of the eighteenth century, a few distinctly Spanish elements had crept into Hopi design repertoire. Filigrees, fleurs-de-lis, bamboo shoot designs, and realistic life forms such as birds, plants, and flowers began to appear.

Cyclic droughts and smallpox epidemics throughout the last half of the eighteenth century and during the nineteenth

E7790

OC2383

See pages 94–99 for captions.

OC1025

century brought the Hopi people in direct contact with the Zuni and Acoma to the east. Virtually abandoning their homes, the Hopi moved in with their relatives to the east for several years at a time. This time was also a period of extensive trade with the groups to the east, and changes brought about through these extensive contacts are evident in the pottery produced at the time.

New design elements, such as filigrees and rosettes, became common in the late eighteenth century Hopi pottery, and the technique of "slipping" (adding a wash of clay to a vessel) reappears after a several-hundred-year absence. The Hopi adopted this technique from the Zuni, and it appears on Hopi pottery after 1780.

During the nineteenth century, the stew bowl, with its strongly flaring rim, became the dominant bowl form. The shape of jars became globular, and they no longer had concave bases. Design layouts continued to reflect older traditions. Stew

OC1041

OC71

bowls were decorated only on the rims; the interior and exterior bottom was plain. As time progressed, design elements became more and more Spanish and the white slip thicker and more crackled. Squash blossoms, animal forms, crooks, volutes, scallops, and arabesques were very common. The interior bottoms of bowls usually were left undecorated although kachina faces were sometimes depicted on stew bowls and plain bowl forms. By the end of the century, stew bowls had less everted rims, jars became even more globular, the crackled slip was thicker, and the designs were identical to those of the Zuni.

Stew bowl rims were decorated with a continuous scallop motif that was either solid, open, or red outlined in black. This same design was modified for the interiors of piki bowls, which appeared as distinct bowl forms at this time. Piki bowl exteriors were almost always left undecorated. During this period, spiral volutes appeared for the first time on interior bowl bottoms and were continued on jars —with even more embellishment. Bird heads and kachina faces were common, and rims almost always painted black.

Up to the end of the nineteenth century, all Hopi pottery, whether decorated or plain, was utilitarian in function and made in every village. It was used to transport and store food and water and in cooking and serving food. The year 1875 marks the beginning of a period in Hopi history and in the history of Hopi pottery in which change becomes constant. Previously, the Hopi had had limited, brief contacts with Americans and Europeans after the first Spanish entrada in 1540. However, in 1875 the first permanent trading post was established by Thomas Varker Keam in a canyon, now known as Keams Canyon, some thirteen miles east of First Mesa.

Keam had a very deep interest in the Hopi people. He became one of the most influential traders in the area and on a number of occasions represented the Hopi people in their dealings with governmental bureaus. A scientist by avocation, "he excavated and catalogued various traditions of prehistoric and early historic ceramic wares" (Wade and McChesney 1980:9). He was instrumental in encouraging the production of ceramics for sale and trade and probably rescued Hopi pottery from total decline in the last years of the nineteenth century. "In the interest of providing the Indians with a possible income and in preserving a vanishing art tradition, Keam encouraged them to manufacture standardized, mass produced bowls, jars and tiles as decorative objects to be sold to tourists" (Wade and McChesney 1980:9).

Jars with sharp shoulders, shallow bowls, vases, globular jars in yellow clay with stylized birds, tails, and wings, were the styles encouraged by Keam. He also encouraged the production of ceramic tiles in a number of geometric and kachina face designs. To facilitate the production of the tiles and to ensure their standardization, Keam issued molds (Wade and McChesney 1981:455).

The effect Thomas Keam had on the production of Hopi pottery can never be measured. It is a foregone conclusion, however, that Keam was the primary figure in the transition from utilitarian ceramic production to an economic-based production. "The history of the southwest Indian art market has shown repeatedly that Pueblo potters are quick to switch styles when cash incentives are offered. At times the mere suggestion of monetary gain is enough to encourage change" (Wade and McChesney 1981:455). It must be remembered that the Hopi were desperately cash poor at this time, and any opportunity to increase buying power at the post was welcomed.

By 1890, Keam had amassed a considerable collection of Hopi material culture items. He and the Scot ethnographer, Alex-

OC217

OC1109

E3007

E8572

E481

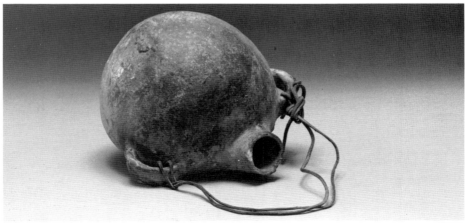

E5233

ander M. Stephen, collected and catalogued over three thousand Hopi baskets, tablettas, and ceremonial items, as well as fifteen hundred ceramic vessels. The Keam Collection, as it is popularly known, was put together at the request of Mary Hemenway of Boston, Massachusetts. Through this collection, we are given the most complete view of turn-of-the-century Hopi ceramics, and the reader is encouraged to see both *America's Great Lost Expedition: The Thomas Keam Collection of Hopi Pottery From the Second Hemenway Expedition, 1890–1894* (Wade and McChesney 1980) and *Historic Hopi Ceramics: The Thomas V. Keam Collection of the Peabody Museum of Archaeology and Ethnology, Harvard University* (Wade and McChesney 1981) for descriptions and photographs of the pottery collected by Thomas Keam.

This was not the only collection amassed by Keam. During these same years, he supplied a number of museums in the United States and abroad with collections of Hopi pottery, both contemporary pieces and prehistoric reproductions. These included the Ethnological Museum in Berlin, the Field Columbian Exposition in Chicago, and the National Museum in Finland. Keam and Stephen were able to obtain well over two thousand pots in only four years. Their offer of trade goods in return for pots must certainly have had an impact on the number of pots produced.

Besides encouraging the production of new shapes, forms, and painting styles, Keam encouraged the women to make reproductions of the prehistoric wares evident in the later prehistoric sites near the First Mesa villages. In fact, Jesse Walker Fewkes, director of the excavation at Sikyatki and director of the Hemenway expedition, mentioned that some of the reproduction pieces were so superb that he worried they might be confused with the real thing (Fewkes 1973:116).

It is not possible from Fewkes' published works to know just how many women were styling prehistoric reproductions for Keam and his collections. According to Wade and McChesney (1981: 455), several different potters were working on the project, and one wonders if Nampeyo might have been one of them. Fewkes also neglected to mention accurately the effect that Keam was having on the Hopi ceramics of this period. "The most notable and damaging oversight to our understanding of the forces shaping the contemporary Hopi society was Fewkes' intentional omission from the historic record of Keam's role in initiating the Sikyatki revival pottery tradition at Hopi" (Wade and McChesney 1980:9). Based on the Keam collection manuscripts, Wade and McChesney are placing the beginning of the revival as early as the 1880s.

Nequatewa states in his biography of Nampeyo that "when she became a young maiden she was as good a potter as any in Walpi, and she did all the decorating for the old lady, her father's mother, a Tewa lady and her teacher, as she had become a good pottery designer." He goes on to say that "when the stores were established on the reservation by the white traders, she was doing a good deal of pottery work, so that when the stores began to trade for pottery, her work was among the best, and she was getting good prices" (Nequatewa 1942). By 1882, Nampeyo and her husband, Leosu, were gathering prehistoric potsherds from nearby sites as inspiration for her designs. "It was in this way that her designs and techniques were developed. Her designs were not all Sikyatki, as so many people thought but were from many ruins, here and there, and thus gave her many ideas" (ibid.).

The story Fewkes put forth is that Nampeyo copied sherds excavated at Sikyatki where her husband, Leosu, was a worker for Fewkes. However, it appears that the exact truth is beyond our grasp since the story now has been clouded in the folklore surrounding Hopi pottery and potters.

OC1096

E149

E507

E6199

E4139

OC1093

What is known about this aspect of Hopi ceramics is the results. Whether Nampeyo saw Sikyatki Polychrome on a number of sites near her home or whether Thomas Keam instituted the concept of prehistoric reproductions is a moot point. By 1900 the predominant pottery type being produced was a yellow ware with black and red painted designs of geometric figures, stylized bird motifs, and kachina faces. The white slipped crackle ware would not be produced in the twentieth century.

In 1898, Nampeyo appeared as a pottery demonstrator in Chicago at the Santa Fe Railway Exhibition. This began her career as pottery demonstrator. She appeared at the Grand Canyon in 1904 and in 1907, and in 1910, she returned to Chicago.

Nampeyo is an example of how popular and saleable Hopi ceramics had become. Pottery was no longer being produced regularly for home use. The trading post, which had sounded the death knell to utilitarian pottery with its enamel and cast iron substitutes, rescued it from oblivion with its promises of goods and money in return. The few utilitarian pieces that were made were stew and piki bowls—both with the traditional Zuni-like designs on yellow ware. However, the production of pottery produced for sale was very brisk.

In 1902, Thomas Varker Keam sold his trading post to the Lorenzo Hubbell family and returned to his native homeland in Cornwall County, England. Hubbell, in turn, sold this post to Joseph Schmedding in 1913. Schmedding's account of the pottery inventory and ease with which he sold it is worth reproducing here:

> While I was familiar with the usual assortment of trade items to be found in trading posts, I was dumbfounded when confronted by Mr. Hubbell's stock of Hopi Indian pottery. He had stored the accumulation of years of trading in a long, shedlike room, putting the pieces as he received them into cases of every shape and size, and when he showed me this immense quantity of pottery there were at least thirty or more large containers filled to the very top. . . .
>
> There must have been tens of thousands of pieces in that lot—I never learned the exact amount. In size and shape they ranged from small pieces of finger-bowl shape to large ollas; others resembled punch bowls and urns, and many pieces were of tall, vaselike appearance. Several large cases were filled with shallow plate-like plaques. All were decorated by hand with the characteristic Hopi designs; many were real show pieces, and of decided artistic value . . .
>
> It was resolved to turn the whole lot over to me at a round sum, a nominal valuation of just a few hundred dollars for all of it. At that offer I agreed, figuring that I should surely be able to turn the pottery at a profit, even if some time might be required to do so.
>
> In that I was not mistaken, as each year at Snake Dance time, the visitors from the outside world would pick up dozens of pieces, to take with them as mementoes of the trip to the Hopi Indians. Throughout the year a steady sale disposed of single pieces, or just a few at a time, to tourists, salesmen, government employees, and others. The biggest sale of pottery, however, was made to B. Altman & Co., New York, whose vice-president came to Keams Canyon one day and bought three thousand assorted pieces, all sizes, leaving the selection to me. That one transaction netted me twice the original cost of the entire stock, and still left thousands of pieces of pottery in my possession. (Schmedding 1951:314–316).

At Oraibi, the location of Lorenzo Hubbell's new trading post, he seems to have amassed another equally large inventory of Hopi pottery. Mrs. White Mountain Smith says that Lorenzo Hubbell, Jr. would take a wagon up to First Mesa and "purchase all the pottery Nampeyo made . . . Fred Harvey was always on the lookout for authentic Indian material and Lorenzo sold him the best of everything he bought" (1940:7).

Keam and Hubbell were not the only traders in the Hopi area. Tom Pavatea, a Hopi trader, had a store at the base of First Mesa where he did a very brisk business in Hopi pottery—selling both to tourists and to businesses in Holbrook (White Mountain Smith 1938:5). Eventually, his business in crafts grew to $25,000 a year (ibid.).

Such indiscriminate buying on the part of the traders and the almost overnight boom in the production of Hopi pottery resulted in the production of a vast number of poorly produced pieces.

In 1922, at the request of the Indian Commissioners, Frank Applegate, Santa Fe artist, spent one summer at First Mesa conducting classes in pottery making for about forty women. He stated that the pottery being produced had "reached such a state that they could sell little of it for two reasons. It broke so easily, and the black paint which they used in painting designs rubbed off if touched" (Applegate 1930). During the period Applegate was at Hopi conducting his pottery classes, he analyzed the clays used and developed a black paint that would not rub off when fired. He determined that the iron oxide and beeweed combination could be improved with the addition of sodium silicate. The new paint solution "probably lasted as long as he was there to supply it," according to Bartlett (1977:13). It seems that he did leave behind one change in pottery production. He is credited with encouraging the production of the tall, high-shouldered vase so popular

before World War II. However, it does not seem that he effected any lasting or obvious change in the quality of pottery produced. Ruth Bunzel did fieldwork with Hopi potters in 1925 and 1926, and her description of pottery at the time is rather bleak:

Hopi pottery is made commercially with the greatest economy of time. For the most part, small pieces are made and enough clay is gathered at one time to make a dozen or more pots. These are molded and set aside to dry and then all are polished and painted together. These factory methods, together with the fact that the trader, himself a Hopi, will buy anything and throw away whatever is too poor for sale, rather than demand better work, combine to produce the worst possible workmanship. The paste is soft—it can be scratched with the fingernail— the pigments are badly prepared and carelessly applied so that the colors soon rub off. The vessels are underfired and the fires so carelessly built that smudging of the vessels almost invariably results (Bunzel 1972:56– 57).

Indeed, Hopi pottery was weathering another decline. Thomas Keam developed a market for Hopi pottery just as the utilitarian-based production became unnecessary because of the availability of manufactured substitutes. Then, this most recent decline, stimulated by an active but indiscriminate market, almost forced Hopi pottery into an irreversible path of cheap tourist trinket production. Another force requiring quality production rather than quantity was soon to exercise its influence on the production of Hopi pottery.

E5369

OC1150

OC1079

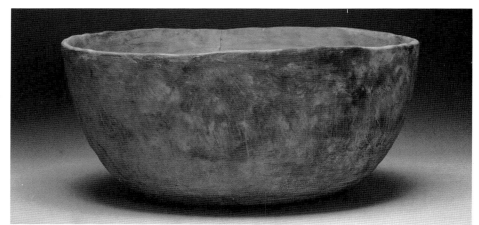

E1305

OC1031

OC1104

OC1078

OC1077

E1116

OC1108

E186

E155

E555

E699

E6387

OC1026

OC1020

OC1072

OC999

OC1082

E5449

OC994

OC1005

OC1060

OC1086

E1261

OC1004

OC482a

OC1071

OC1018

E7660

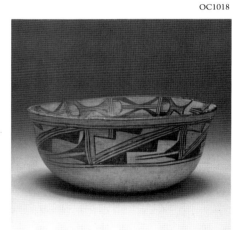

OC1013

E5220

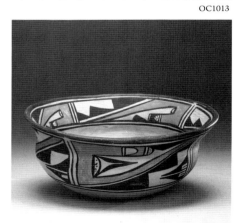

OC1000

OC1050

OC1089

OC1091

E5222

OC1014

OC1017

E5451

OC2734J

E7388

OC1036

OC1028

E2365

E5406

E4203

OC214

E853

E410

E4443

OC1840

E372

E2006

E2243

E215

E7572

E770

E433

E434

COLOR PORTFOLIO

E380

E859

OC1054

OC1055

E7234

OC1051

OC2166

OC1076

E805

E815

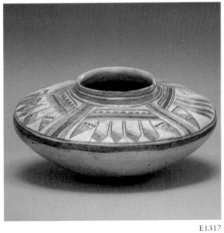

E1317

OC1059

OC21a

E73

E25h E25c E25i E25f
E836 E25d E25a E828

OC1058

E7380

E7381

E74

E7662

E7567

E7573

OC1075

E2366

E76

OC1069

E78

E466

E7678

E79

E7664

E7656

E156

E855

E5393
E7644

E5391
E818

E458

56

E2585

E2591
E1408

E1407
E7632

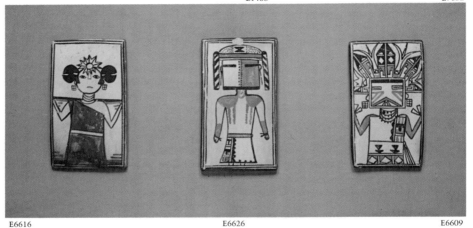

E6616

E6626

E6609

E5353

E7448

E2941

E2943

E198

E1411

E2940

E1419

E2630

E245

E431

E496

E450

E523

E522

E553

E611

E972

E1417

E3447

E1465

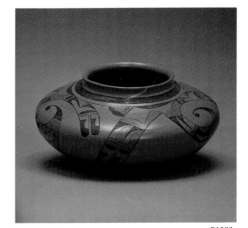

E1503

E8008a,b

E2207

E2208

E2241

E5752

E5750

E2638a,b

E2641

E1916   E3124   E1919
E2582   E1915

E3314

E4166

E5100

E5773

E5898

E6352

E6355

E6356

E6366

E5370

E7802

E8398

E8756

E438

OC2784

E196

E187

E1412

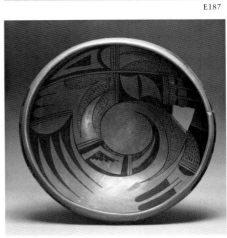

E199

THE HOPI CRAFTSMAN EXHIBITION

In early 1930, Mary-Russell Ferrell Colton, co-founder of the Museum of Northern Arizona, set out to rescue Hopi pottery from oblivion. She felt that no one on the reservation was encouraging the production of quality work, that mediocrity was acceptable, and that no one was educating the buying public on what constituted good Hopi art. This self-perpetuating problem could only result in the eventual death of Hopi crafts.

Her solution to the problem was to organize at the Museum of Northern Arizona an annual exhibition and sale of the best available Hopi crafts and hold it during the week of July 4—Flagstaff's heaviest tourist season. She believed that this would encourage Hopi artists to produce their best work and, at the same time, educate the buying public about good Hopi art.

Mary-Russell Ferrell Colton went another step further in ensuring the success of her plan. She set up the exhibit as a juried show and offered cash prizes to the artists for the best objects in various categories. She was well aware that the buying public responded positively to the concept of "blue ribbon" pieces and that cash incentives to the potters, in what was at that time an almost cash-free cul-

ture, would work together for a positive outcome.

By March of 1930, Mary-Russell Ferrell Colton had her plan so firmly defined that she went out to the reservation to discuss the concept of the exhibition with the superintendent of the Hopi reservation. With his blessing, she and museum employees Lyndon Lane Hargrave and Edmond Nequatewa visited each village (except Polacca which was quarantined because of meningitis) and presented the concept of an exhibition and sale. She explained, with Nequatewa interpreting, why the Museum of Northern Arizona wanted to do the show, how it would benefit the craftsmen, how prizes would be determined, and how the individuals would be paid. The Hopi were apparently quite taken with the idea. The Anglo traders, however, did not quite agree:

We met a friendly opposition from Lorenzo Hubbell, Jr. (trader at Kyakotsmovi). He takes the attitude that it will be detrimental to the trader to raise the standard of Indian art work, as the customer will then desire only the finest pieces and there will be little sale for the mediocre stuff.

We take the stand and firmly believe that it is *absolutely necessary* for the

E157

E5404

trader, as well as for the Indian artist, to keep up a high standard of workmanship.

It is true that the tourist customer will buy once a bowl which looks well when he makes the purchase, but when he takes it home, does he feel cheated when the beautiful design rubs off? Will he return again and again for such an article? How will he feel when he happily carries home a wedding belt and afterwards finds that it is not like the beautiful old one in the museum, it is woven and not plaited; his striped bed blanket is a coarse crooked thing and the colors are muddy; the wedding dress is woven of ordinary cotton string and not of soft, creamy white handspun yarn; his baskets are so very different too—the weaving is so coarse, the colors fade, and the rims are casually attached. Will this customer return?

I say (that) unless the traders get behind *better workmanship* this unavoidable comparison is going to be a detriment to the trader. (We should) see that better things are made and (both Indians and traders) get better prices for them.

All art has a tendency to degenerate —to go downhill; it needs jacking up and practical encouragement. This is just the movement we are trying to start; we have no desire to step on anyone's toes. We are scientific and artistic, not commercial. We have no desire to undercut prices or to go into the selling end of the proposition more than absolutely necessary (Colton 1930a).

In the first Hopi Craftsman Exhibition (held only four months after the first exploratory trip), forty-nine pots were selected for inclusion in the sale; of these, forty-six sold. By the second exhibition, ninety-nine pots were entered and ninety sold. By the second year, Mary-Russell Ferrell Colton was encouraging potters and others to identify their works in some manner. It was her goal to help the craftsmen develop a steady clientele. She suggested that the interpreter explain that "the Museum wishes to build up the individual reputations of the craftsmen, so

that people coming to the exhibition each year will ask for baskets of so-and-so and the weaving and pottery of such-and-such, a craftsman. Interpreter will tell the people that Mrs. Colton and the Museum strongly urge every craftsman to put *his* or *her mark* or *name* on every piece of their work. In this way, the people that buy will remember them and come to know their work" (Colton 1931).

By 1932, the rules and explanations to the craftsmen included more directions and statements detailing what types of crafts the museum wanted and the quality that was mandatory:

> Potters! Use care and see that your *designs do not rub off.* We cannot accept pottery with designs that rub off. Make *old shapes* of pottery for the exhibition (Colton 1932).

The museum encouraged the reproductions of old plainware storage jars and canteens. Although canteens were popular among the buying public and were made regularly, the large storage jars were not popular with the potters. In a letter to the National Association of Indian Affairs, Mary-Russell Ferrell Colton (1933) states:

> When the Museum began its work with the Hopi, the manufacture of the old utility wares was rapidly becoming a lost art. These plain, unpolished wares in the past have been made in large decorative forms. The Museum is using every effort to encourage the revival of the manufacture of these things, but is encountering considerable difficulty because, in many cases, points in the technique have been lost. However, several potters are striving to produce these wares and in the last years some very large forms have been produced.

Even though this aspect of the museum's work with Hopi potters was never totally successful, the museum did encourage the development of new forms of art with purely Hopi design motifs and the application of old arts to modern uses.

In a *Christian Science Monitor* article dated July 1, 1937, Mary-Russell Ferrell Colton attests to the success of the museum's project: "At First Mesa the women who make pottery relate with pride how they have orders from people in 'far away' places in the United States; containing requests for their work, and parties have come directly to their homes to buy their ceramics; this is because the individual's role as well as the tribal reputation of the Hopis is always stressed at the Hopi Craftsman."

By this date, the exhibition had become a "tradition" among the Hopi participants and the museum's public as well. In the 1939 exhibition, one hundred ninety-seven pots were entered and one hundred eighty-two sold. Looking back over the first decade of the exhibition, Harold S. Colton reflected on the experience: "It was designed as a living ethnologic problem and has been carried out under the supervision of the Museum of Northern Arizona. It represents an intensive effort to maintain, improve, and create a market for the arts and crafts of a single people " (Colton 1939).

Indeed, the exhibition was so successful that it endured the Depression and total closure during World War II (from 1943 to 1946 no exhibitions were held). When it reopened in 1947, the number of pots entered and sold was comparable to previous years. In fact, the success was to continue through the 1950s and 1960s. From 1930 to 1975, the museum averaged about eighty-nine percent of entered ceramics sold. From 1976 to the present, the percentage has fallen to sixty-nine percent of entered ceramics sold. The reasons for this decline in numbers are complex. The museum's records from the show indicate substantial increases in prices of pots in just one year from 1975 to 1976.

The success of the Hopi Craftsman Exhibition cannot be judged solely on the percentages of entries sold. Sales was only one aspect of the Coltons' goals for the show; creativity and growth were also important.

Many new forms of vessels were developed during the mid-twentieth century. These new forms had no roots in Hopi culture and were strictly Anglo-inspired. Coffee and tea canisters (constructed in the traditional manner with Hopi designs); fruitbowls, bowls in the forms of handled baskets, and lidded jars made to look like chickens were all popular items. Soon special orders for items made specifically for an individual's special needs were part of a potter's repertoire. Unfortunately, some of the pieces produced were not as sophisticated as others, in execution of either concept or design, and reflected poorly on the reputation of Hopi pottery. Ceramic ashtrays in the forms of cowboy hats and spurs or salt and pepper shakers were made for the increasing tourist industry and furthered a stereotyped image of Native American arts and crafts. Still, other potters relished in the newfound freedom of contemporary Hopi ceramics unconstrained by tradition or function. These ladies combined their traditional sense of design and technology and added their own individual treatments and created new design elements or gave old designs a new, more contemporary application.

Polished redware bowls and jars soon became common and were never executed with more style and grace than by Garnet Pavatea, long-time demonstrator at the Hopi Craftsman Exhibition. A special addition to her redware pieces was a punctate band around the necks of jars and the mouths of bowls. This design was effected by pressing the tip of a triangular-shaped bottle opener onto the surface of the undried vessel. Still others perfected other plainware styles. Elizabeth White, a Third Mesa potter from Kyakotsmovi, developed an unpainted cream-colored style with stylized corn cobs made through a technique similar to embossing or re-

E459

E469

E5224

E612

E2603

E2604

E7863

poussé embellishing the jars. This same technique and the use of stylized corn is being produced by Elizabeth White's nephew Al Qöyawayma of Scottsdale, Arizona. The polished plainware styles lend themselves to elegant but simple forms: jars, vases, and high-shouldered seed jars are not unusual.

In the painted wares, the traditional black and red on yellow, which ranges from pale yellow or white through to orange, is still popular among potters and consumers. The technique developed in late prehistoric times and perfected by those like Nampeyo is still most representative of Hopi pottery. Nampeyo's descendants have perfected this particular technique to a state that is rarely equaled. During the twentieth century, though other color combinations were developed, black-and-white painted designs on red backgrounds became popular. Pots with a painted black design on red background on the vessel's exterior combined with painted black designs on white background on the interior (black on red and black on white) became common. Although only a few potters worked in this style, its effect is quite striking. The stark, white-slipped pottery popularized and perfected by the Naha and Navasie families has been duplicated by many. Historically, the Hopi learned the white-slip technique from their Zuni relatives —and it was this slipped crackle ware that was replaced by Nampeyo and others working around the turn of the century. This more recently successful technique, which began in the 1950s, was dependent on the development of a suitable slip material—kaolin clay.

In all the painting styles, certain forms predominate. Low, shallow bowls with designs painted on the interior; high, rounded-shouldered, narrow-mouth seed jars; high, sharp-shouldered, narrow-mouth jars and vases and tiles are all relatively new forms as is the handled, double-spouted jar commonly called the "wedding" vase. Piki or mixing bowls, stew or serving bowls, canteens, and ladles are all very old forms produced today with contemporary designs.

Designs, continuing an ancient tradition, have become more and more stylized and sophisticated. Birds, commonly encountered in Hopi pottery, are sometimes depicted realistically but are most often stylized. Beaks and birds' heads are encountered regularly as are stylized wings, tails, and feathers. These designs are first seen in late prehistoric wares known as Sikyatki Polychrome; later, when Nampeyo and others reestablished the style, it was referred to as the Sikyatki Revival. Almost as common, however, is the use of bands of geometric designs: triangles (both pendant and dependant), hatching lines, scrolls, volutes, and arabesques. Continuing the tradition set late in the nineteenth century, Hopi potters also use kachina faces, rain clouds, and tadpoles to decorate bowl interiors and some jar exteriors. The mosquito, a design known from earlier times, is now becoming a common element on pottery. When the Keam Collection of Historic Hopi Ceramics traveled in the Southwest, a number of Hopi potters saw either the show or its catalog. A number of vessels made subsequent to the show incorporated design elements, such as the mosquito, seen in the historic pieces (Allen, field notes).

As documented in the historic development of Hopi ceramics and as indicated in the trends seen in contemporary works, forms and designs need not have their roots in Hopi culture, but as the forms become adopted and adapted to the art, they become embellished and amended, to become truly Hopi designs.

There is no technique for measuring the actual effect of the Hopi Craftsman Exhibition on Hopi crafts. It is possible, however, to gauge the success of Mary-Russell Ferrell Colton's goals. A wider and more stable market for Hopi crafts

E7864

E615

E947

E5225

E5227

E1466

has been established. Today, visits to galleries in the Southwest and the East and West coasts, and a quick perusal of advertisements in related magazines attest to the popularity of Hopi crafts. Moreover, the names of individual artists recognized for the quality of their works are often well known. It is not possible to know whether the Hopi Craftsman Exhibition "saved" any craft from extinction. But without a utilitarian or ceremonial reason to continue producing an item, people will not produce it. The Hopi Craftsman Exhibition was developed at a time when a number of objects were being re-placed with commercially made products. The replacement of functional production with economic-based production almost certainly had some effect on keeping crafts alive.

The future of the Hopi Craftsman Exhibition is only as sound as the future of Hopi craftwork. Our obligation is not to the past but to the future—both to the crafts being produced and the artists producing them. Our goal for the next fifty years should be simple: encourage individual expression through Hopi art forms and Hopi motifs while maintaining the best in quality and workmanship.

E2219

E3311

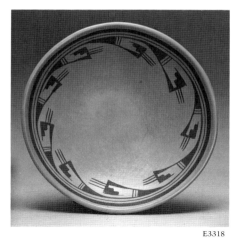

E3318

E3456

E3694

E4212

E2505

E5753

E7871

E5963

E4224B

E4224A

E3849

E1923

E8422

E6364

OC1007

E2944

E428

E1414

E432

E454

E440

E427

E1316

E7423a–e

E439

E2641

E8423

E8599

E8388

E6675

E185

E8007

E8289

E6650

E3017

E3695

E5780

E5491a–c

E6130

E8529   E8575

AFTERWORD

Only time can answer the questions of the future of Hopi ceramics. However, several trends seem clear.

The Hopi people are not isolated from the outside world and have the same options available to them as any other craftsmen. Neither the availability of commercially processed clays and paints nor the option of kiln-firing is to be ignored. These are all time-saving devices that maximize production. However, it is obvious that some elements will be sacrificed at the expense of these new developments. Just how these changes might affect the market for and marketability of Hopi ceramics is uncertain.

Hopi pottery is a vital craft—and production seems vigorous. Today, pottery production is not limited just to women. Beginning with Charles Loloma's pottery production in the 1950s, men have produced pottery in increasing numbers. Although they are not producing the traditional bowl and jar forms, their sculptural pieces are adding a new, fresh dimension to contemporary Hopi ceramics.

It seems likely that ceramic production will continue to be grouped in the three broad categories evidenced since prehistoric times: some pieces will be poorly designed and poorly made; most will be technologically and aesthetically balanced; and only a few pieces will combine technological sophistication with the spirit and essence of Hopi culture and capture the vitality of this centuries-old Hopi pottery tradition.

The Museum of Northern Arizona has supported this work in the hope that its historical perspective will increase readers' appreciation for the pots they own or may someday own. For the Hopi potters, it is hoped that this production will document the work done in years gone by and provide stimulation for those pieces yet to come. Mutual respect between the consumer and producer can only create a positive future.

"The Museum of Northern Arizona believes that the Indian has an important contribution to make toward our mutual civilization—his art, unique and beautiful, purely American—is a direct link with the prehistoric past. He is a creator of design and a master of abstract form . . ." (Colton 1930b).

PHOTO CAPTIONS

Hopi Pottery, pages 13–47

E7790 A Plainware scoop dating from the 1600s that possibly was used for stirring drying ground corn in a container over a fire

OC2383 Geometric designs of black and red on an orange gourd-shaped ladle (1700–1800)

OC1025 Geometric design in black and red on an orange ladle (1800–1820)

OC1041 Geometric design in black and red on a white ladle. Note wear along lip (1800–1830)

OC71 Geometric design in black and red on white ladle (1800–1840)

OC217 Geometric design in black and red on white ladle (1800–1840)

OC1109 A Plainware scoop made by the mother of contemporary potter Susie at Oraibi (1900–1910)

E3007 A Hu kachina effigy handle on a black on white ladle with tadpole motifs (1870–1910)

E8572 Basketry impressed bottom Plainware dipper made by Vera Pooyouma at Hotevilla (1981)

E481 A pitched canteen by Tewavensi at Hotevilla (1935).

E5233 A pitched canteen (1850–1900)

OC1096 A pitched canteen made by Hunimimka at Hotevilla (1908–1910)

E149 A pitched canteen (1931)

E507 A "personal-size" pitched canteen (1939)

E6199 A "personal-size" pitched canteen made by Vera Pooyouma at Hotevilla (1973)

E4139 A Plainware bowl (1700)

OC1093 A Plainware utilitarian jar (1700–1800)

E5369 A fillet-rimmed Plainware jar with indented base for placement in wood cookstove eye, made by Sekayumka at Moencopi (pre-1850)

OC1150 A Plainware bowl made by Talashoynum at Oraibi (1850)

OC1079 A Plainware teakettle made by Tyvewynka at Shungopovi (1887–1890)

E1305 Basketry impressed bottom Plainware bowl owned by Tewaquaptewa's grandmother in Oraibi (1850–1900)

OC1031 Basketry impressed bottom Redware bowl (1850–1900)

OC1104 A Plainware storage jar that may have been used as an indigo dye pot (1880)

OC1078 A Plainware tea kettle made by Qumanquimka at Shungopovi (1895)

OC1077 A Plainware utilitarian orange bowl that has been mended (1900)

E1116 A Plainware boot-shaped cooking jar (1900–1953)

OC1108 Basketry impressed bottom Redware mixing bowl made by Mabel Tcosytiwa's mother at Hotevilla (1928)

E186 A Plainware boot-shaped cooking jar from Oraibi (1931)

E155 A Plainware pitched storage jar made by Cyashongka at Hotevilla (1935)

E555 An orange Plainware utilitarian bowl made by Siwirinepnina at Hotevilla (1939)

E699 Basketry impressed Plainware storage jar by Sinimpka at Hotevilla (1942)

E6387 A thumb-impressed Plainware jar made by Vera Pooyouma at Hotevilla (1973)

OC1026 Black and red geometric designs on a white serving bowl (1800–1850)

OC1020 Black and red geometric designs on an orange serving bowl (1800–1850)

OC1072 Black and red geometric designs on a yellow serving bowl (1800–1850)

OC999 Black and red fleur-de-lis and arabesque designs on a yellow serving bowl (1840–1870)

OC1082 Black and red geometric and arabesque designs on a yellow serving bowl (1840–1870)

E5449 Black and red arabesque designs on an orange serving bowl (1840–1880)

OC994 Black and red geometric and arabesque designs on a yellow serving bowl (1850–1870)

OC1005 Black and white and black and red geometric designs on a white serving bowl (1860–1880)

OC1060 Black and red geometric designs on a yellow serving bowl (1850–1900)

OC1086 Black and red geometric designs on a yellow serving bowl with a red slipped base (1860–1880)

E1261 Black and red geometric designs on a white serving bowl (1870–1900)

OC1004 Black and red arabesque designs on an orange serving bowl (1870–1900)

OC482a Black and red arabesque designs on a white serving bowl (1870–1900)

OC1071 Black and red geometric and arabesque designs on a yellow serving bowl (1870–1900)

OC1018 Black and red geometric designs on a yellow serving bowl (1880–1910)

E7660 Black on yellow and black and red geometric designs on a yellow serving bowl (1885–1920)

OC1013 Black and red geometric designs on a yellow serving bowl (1900)

E5220 Black and white and black and red geometric and arabesque designs on a yellow serving bowl (1900–1930)

OC1000 Black and red geometric designs on a yellow serving bowl (1900–1930)

OC1050 Black and red arabesque designs and flower motifs on a yellow mixing bowl (1870–1900)

OC1089 Black and red arabesque designs on a yellow mixing bowl (1870–1900)

OC1091 Geometric designs in black and red on a yellow mixing bowl made by Emma's grandmother at Oraibi (1885–1915)

E5222 An orange piki bowl with black arabesque designs (1880–1900)

OC1014 Black and red arabesque and geometric designs decorate a yellow serving bowl (1870–1900)

OC1017 A black on white piki bowl with a geometric motif (1890–1910)

E5451 A red piki bowl with a black arabesque design (1900–1930)

OC2734j An arabesque design on a black on yellow mixing bowl (1930)

OC1036 Geometric designs in black and red on a white bowl (1800–1840)

OC1028 A yellow bowl decorated in black and red with floral and bird motifs (1830–1870)

E2365 A black stylized bird graces a white bowl with a footed base (1880–1900)

E5046 A black and red Salako kachina motif decorates this white bowl (1850–1880)

E4203 Black and red geometric designs on a white bowl (1800–1870)

E1482 Geometric designs in black and red decorate a yellow jar with a footed base with kick-up (1700–1730)

OC1074 Stylized black and red bird designs are depicted on a yellow jar (1900–1920)

OC214 A black on white handled jar has an unidentified kachina motif with sun (1900–1930)

E853 Black and red zoomorphs and cloud symbols decorate a white jar (1918)

E410 An orange jar with black stylized bird designs from Shungopovi. The jar's rim shows wear. (1920–1923)

E4443 A white bowl decorated with black and red stylized bird designs (1880–1890)

OC1840 A yellow bowl with a black and red stylized bird and geometric rim design (1900–1930)

E372 An orange bowl with black geometric designs (1901)

E2006 A black and red zoomorphic figure on a yellow bowl (1910–1920)

E2243 An orange bowl with black and red stylized bird motifs and a lug handle on the rim (1925–1930)

E215 An orange bowl designed with black and red stylized birds and exhibiting prefire perforations in the bottom, created by Nampeyo. Tewa (1920–1930)

E7572 A black and white stylized bird on a red jar, production attributed to Nampeyo. Tewa (1904–1915)

E770 A black stylized bird design on a yellow jar purchased from Tom Pavatea's store. Nampeyo. Tewa (1900–1921)

E433 A yellow jar decorated with a black and red stylized bird design made by Fannie Polacca Nampeyo. Tewa (1922)

E434 Black and red stylized bird designs adorn this yellow jar made by Siayowsi. First Mesa (1922)

Color Portfolio, pages 48–64

E380 Geometric design executed in black and red on white (1800–1850)

E859 Black and red floral motifs on an orange jar (1870–1900)

OC1054 Black and red arabesque designs on a white jar (1870–1900)

OC1055 Black and red arabesque and geometric designs on an orange jar (1870–1900)

E7234 Black and red volute and arabesque designs on a yellow jar (1880–1890)

OC2166 Black and red volute and geometric designs on a white jar (1880–1900)

OC1076 Black geometric designs on a yellow jar (1880–1900)

TILES:

E805 Two turkey heads with cloud symbols (1890–1900)

E815 Hu′ kachina design (1890–1900)

E1317 Black and red stylized bird designs on a yellow jar (1890–1920)

OC1059 Black and red volutes and geometric designs on a white jar (1890–1920)

OC21a Black and red stylized bird designs on a white jar (1880–1920)

E73 Black and red stylized bird designs on a yellow jar (1880–1930)

TILES:

E25h Male figure—possibly Jessie Walter Fewkes (1897)

E25c Talavai kachina design (1897)

E25i Man on horseback (1897)

E25f Geometric design—possibly a dance wand representation (1897)

E836 Koyemsi design (1890–1900)

E25d Tawa kachina design (1897)

E25g Floral designs (1897)

E828 Nuvakachina design (1890–1900)

OC1058 Black and red geometric designs on a white jar (1900)

E7380 Black and red stylized bird designs on a yellow jar (1890–1900)

E7381 Black and red stylized bird designs on an orange jar (1900)

E74 Black and red stylized bird designs on a white jar (1900)

E7662 Black and red stylized bird designs on an orange jar (1900–1910)

E7567 Black geometric designs on a white canteen (1900–1915)

E7573 Geometric bird design done in a non-Hopi style. The piece features black and white on red and is attributed to Nampeyo. (1900–1915)

OC1081 Plainware canteen (1900–1920)

OC1075 Black and red kachina figures on an orange jar (1900–1920)

E2366 Yellow pitcher with punctate and black geometric designs (1900–1920)

E76 Black and red stylized bird designs on a white jar by Nampeyo at Tewa (1900–1930)

OC1069 Black and red stylized bird on a white jar (1900–1930)

E78 Black bird design on a yellow jar (1900–1930)

E466 Black and red stylized bird design on a yellow jar by Leona Polacca at Tewa (1900–1930)

E7678 Black and red stylized bird designs on a white jar by Nampeyo at Tewa (1900–1930)

E79 Black stylized bird design on a yellow jar (1900–1930)

E7664 Black and red stylized bird design on a white jar by Nampeyo at Tewa (1910–1930)

E7656 Black and white geometric design on a red jar (1910–1930)

E156 Black stylized bird design on a yellow jar by Nampeyo at Tewa (1912)

E855 Black and white bird design on a red jar attributed to Nampeyo at Tewa (1918)

TILES:

E5393 Salako kachina design (1918)

E5391 Salako mana kachina design (1918)

E7644 Angakachina design (1910–1930)

E818 Salako kachina design (1890–1900)

E458 Black geometric and curvilinear designs on an orange jar, Walpi (1925–1935)

E2585 Black and red kachina figure on a yellow jar (1930)

TILES:

E2591 Bird motif by Sadie Adams at Tewa (1930)

E1407 Stylized bird motif by Sadie Adams at Tewa (1930–1945)

E1408 Kipok kachina design by Sadie Adams of Tewa (1930–1945)

E7632 Tasap Yeibechai kachina motif (1910–1930)

TILES:

E6616 Powamuymana figure (1930–1960)

E6626 Hemis kachina design (1940–1960)

E6609 Palhikmana kachina design (1900–1930)

E5353 Black and red stylized bird designs on a white jar (1930–1940)

E7448 Black and red stylized bird design on a yellow jar (1930–1970)

E2941 Black and red stylized bird design on a yellow jar by Paqua Naha (1931–1953)

E2943 Black and red stylized bird design on a yellow jar by Poolisie of Sichomovi (1933)

E198 Black geometric and arabesque designs on a red jar (1934)

E1411 Black and red stylized bird designs on a yellow jar by Nampeyo and Fannie Polacca Nampeyo at Tewa (1934)

E2940 Black and red stylized bird designs on a yellow jar by Poolisie of Sichomovi (1935)

E1419 Black and red stylized bird designs on a yellow jar by Paqua Naha of Tewa (1935)

E2630 Black and red stylized bird design on a yellow jar by Nampeyo and Fannie Polacca Nampeyo of Polacca (1935)

E245 Black and red stylized birds on a yellow jar by Fannie Polacca Nampeyo at Polacca (1936)

E431 Black and red stylized bird design on a yellow jar by Sadie Adams of Tewa (1936)

E496 Black and red geometric designs on a yellow jar by Chorosie at Tewa (1937)

E450 Black geometric designs on a yellow jar by Tewanginema of Sichomovi (1938)

E523 Black stylized bird design on a red jar by Paqua Naha, Tewa (1939)

E522 Black geometric designs on a yellow jar by Tewanginema at Sichomovi (1939)

E553 Black geometric designs on a yellow bowl by Tewanginema at Sichomovi (1939)

E611 Black geometric designs on a yellow jar by Betty Harvey at Tewa (1940)

E972 Black geometric design on a red jar by Kate Seeni of Walpi (1948)

E1417 Black and red stylized bird designs on a white jar by Mrs. Willie Healing (Annie Nampeyo) at Tewa (1950)

E3447 Black and red stylized bird design on a yellow jar by Daisy Nampeyo, Polacca (1950)

E1465 Black and white geometric design on a red jar by Garnet Pavatea, Tewa (1958)

E1503 Black stylized bird design on a red jar by Garnet Pavatea, Tewa (1959)

E8008a, b Black and red geometric design executed on an orange jar by Laura Tamosie of Tewa (1959–1961)

E2207 Black and red stylized bird design on a white jar by Lena Charlie, Tewa (1960)

E2208 Black stylized bird design on a red jar by Garnet Pavatea of Tewa (1960)

E2241 Black and red stylized bird design executed on an orange canteen by Norma Ami, Sichomovi (1961)

E5752 Black and red stylized bird designs on a yellow jar by Fannie Polacca Nampeyo at Polacca (1962–1972)

E5750 Black and red stylized bird designs on a yellow jar by Leah Nampeyo, Polacca (1962–1972)

E2638a, b Redware jar by Violet Huma at Sichomovi (1963)

E2641 Black and black and red stylized bird and geometric designs on a yellow serving bowl by Rena Kavena, Sichomovi (1963)

TILES:

E1916 Stylized bird motif by Laura Tamosie, Tewa (1964)

E3124 Stylized bird motif by Carol Namoki, Tewa (1965)

E1919 Stylized bird motif by Laura Tamosie, Tewa (1964)

E2582 Geometric design by Sadie Adams, Tewa (1930)

E1915 Stylized bird motif by Laura Tamosie, Tewa (1964)

E3314 Punctate Redware jar by Clara Peesha, Sichomovi (1966)

E4166 Repoussé corn motif on a Plainware jar by Elizabeth White, Kyakotsmovi (1969)

E5100 Plainware repoussé cornmaiden wind bell by Elizabeth White of Kyakotsmovi (1970)

E5773a, b Black and red stylized birds on a white jar by Emogene Lomakema of Walpi (1972)

E5898a, b Black and red stylized bird design on a yellow jar by Nettie Ami, Sichomovi (1972)

E6352 Black and red stylized bird designs on a white jar by Tonita Hamilton Nampeyo, Polacca (1973)

E6355 Black and red stylized bird designs on a white jar by Nellie Nampeyo Douma at Polacca (1973)

E6356 Black and red stylized bird design on a white jar by Priscilla Namingha Nampeyo, Polacca (1973)

E6366 Black and red geometric design on a white jar by Marie Nampeyo Koopee, Polacca (1973)

E5370 Black and red stylized bird design on an orange jar by Lorna Lomakema, Tewa (1974)

E7802 Black geometric design on a red jar by Evelyn Poolheco, Walpi (1977)

E8398 Redware jar with repoussé corn by Al Qöyawayma, Scottsdale (1978)

E8756 Black and red stylized bird design on a white wedding jar by Helen Naha, Tewa (1983)

The Hopi Craftsman Exhibition, pages 67–89

E438 Stylized bird designs in black and red on a yellow jar (1925–1935)

OC2784 Stylized bird designs combine with geometric motifs in black on a red bowl (1930)

E196 Black and red geometric designs adorn an orange bowl (1931)

E187 A black stylized bird and a scalloped rim decorate a red bowl made by Theresa Harvey at Walpi (1931)

E1412 A white bowl embellished with black and red stylized bird designs, made by Tewanginema at Sichomovi (1900–1933)

E199 A black stylized bird decorates a red bowl made by Tewanginema at Sichomovi (1933)

E157 An orange bowl decorated with black and red stylized bird motifs and geometric designs, made by Susie Bacon at Sichomovi (1935)

E5404 A yellow bowl with a black zoomorphic design made by Flora Ray at Tewa (1936)

E459 Black and white geometric designs decorate a red jar made by Kochahonawe at Walpi (1936)

E469 A white bowl adorned with a black and red stylized bird design made by Siayowsi at Tewa (1938)

E5224 A Heheya kachina motif decorates this bowl with opposing perforations at each side for hanging. Made by Emma Heyah at Walpi (1930–1950). Note its similarity to E5225, p. 75.

E612 Black and red geometric designs ornament a yellow jar made by Matilda Williams at Sichomovi (1940)

E2603, E2604 Two tan bowls adorned with red and black oil base paints in geometric designs over traditional black and red on yellow. The repainting is Hopi. (1942)

E7863, E7864 Two yellow lamps with black and red stylized birds by Sadie Adams at Tewa (1930–1940)

E615 A white bowl decorated in a black and red curvilinear winged design made by Fannie Polacca Nampeyo at Tewa (1930–1940)

E947 Black and red geometric stepped motifs and a Mexican mask decorate an orange bowl made by Fannie Polacca Nampeyo at Tewa (1940–1952)

E5225 A white bowl with black and red Heheya katsinmana motif, with perforations on two sides for hanging, made by Garnet Pavatea at Tewa (1954). Note similarity to E5224, p. 71.

E5227 A black and red bird on a white bowl by Ella Tiwa at Sichomovi (1954)

E1466 Black and white stylized birds and curvilinear border on red bowl, by Garnet Pavatea at Tewa (1958)

E2219 A white-handled bowl decorated with black stylized birds made by Garnet Pavatea at Tewa (1961)

E3311 Black stylized bird designs on a white interior and black geometric designs on the red exterior of a bowl by Marsha Fritz at Sichomovi (1966)

E3318 Black geometric designs on a red bowl made by Ethel Youvella at Tewa (1966)

E3456 Stylized birds in black on a white bowl made by Helen Naha at Tewa (1967)

E3694 Black stylized bird designs on a white interior and black geometric designs on a red exterior are featured on a bowl made by Emogene Lomakema at Walpi (1968)

E4212 A black kachina motif on a white interior and black geometric designs on a red exterior on a bowl made by Carol Namoki at Polacca (1969)

E2505 An orange bowl is decorated with a black and red kachina motif (1960–1970)

E5753 Stylized wings in black and red grace a yellow jar made by Fannie Polacca Nampeyo at Tewa (1962–1972)

E7871 A red wedding jar decorated with a black stylized bird made by Nancy Lewis of Sichomovi (1971)

E5963 A black and red stylized bird adorns a white wedding jar made by Carol Namoki of Tewa (1973)

E8765 A red mold-made vase by Nan Talahongva is ornamented in black paint with a stylized bird/zoomorph (1980)

E4224b A polished Brownware ladle that misfired during a rainshower in the firing process; the piece was intended to be Redware. Made by Garnet Pavatea of Tewa. See E4224a, E3849. (1968)

E4224a A polished Brownware bowl was intended to be Redware but misfired because of rain during the firing process. Made by Garnet Pavatea of Tewa. (1968)

E3849 A punctate design distinguishes this polished Brownware bowl which was fired with the bowl described as E4224a—hence, the unusual color. Made by Garnet Pavatea of Tewa. (1968)

E1923 A Plainware vase made by Louise Nahsongya at Sichomovi (1964)

E8422 A Whiteware, basketry impressed bowl made by Elizabeth White at Kyakotsmovi (1979)

E6364 A distinctive design is achieved for a polished Redware bowl by adorning it with shells and feathers. Made by Dextra Qüotskuyva Nampeyo at Polacca. (1973)

OC1007 Black geometric designs on a yellow mixing bowl (1890–1910)

E2944 Black and red colors fashioned the Salakomana kachina motif on a yellow mixing bowl made by Charlotte Pala at Tewa (1930)

E428 A yellow mixing bowl is designed with a Salakomana kachina motif using black and red colors by Charlotte Pala at Tewa (1931)

E1414 A mixing bowl with a red exterior and yellow interior is designed in black and red with stylized bird designs and tadpoles by Tewanginema at Sichomovi (1933)

E432 A combination of arabesque and geometric designs in black adds distinction on a yellow mixing bowl made by Poolisie at Sichomovi (1934)

E454 A yellow mixing bowl is enhanced with the black and red arabesque and geometric designs created by Poolisie at Sichomovi (1938)

E440 A white piki bowl decorated with black and red arabesque designs by Mrs. Keely at Tewa (1930–1940)

E427 Black and red stylized bird motifs on an orange mixing bowl made by Tewanginema at Sichomovi (1938)

E1316 Black geometric designs grace the upper outer edge of a red mixing bowl made by Garnet Pavatea at Tewa (1956)

E7423a–e A polished Redware bowl and ladles are used to serve blue marble dumplings. Made by Vivian Mumzewa at Sichomovi. (1976)

E439 Black and red geometric and arabesque designs add distinction to a yellow serving bowl made by Ella Tiwa at Sichomovi (1935)

E2641 Black and red geometric designs enhance an orange serving bowl made by Rena Kavena at Sichomovi (1963)

E8423 An orange serving bowl is distinguished with black and red geometric designs by Rena Kavena at Sichomovi (1977)

E8599 A geometric design in black and red borders an orange service bowl made by Marcella Kahe at Sichomovi (1982)

E8388 A white scoop takes on a dramatic look with a black and red geometric design, made by Juanita Healing at Tewa (1979)

E6675 A yellow pitcher is enhanced with black geometric designs (1924)

E185 Black and white stylized bird designs enhance a red ashtray (1933)

E8007 Yellow hat effigy ashtray with black geometric designs (1930–1950)

E8289 Black geometric designs adorn a white lampshade (1940–1960)

E6650 A white matchholder is decorated with a black geometric design (1940–1960)

E3017 Koyemsi effigy Plainware windbell by Elizabeth White at Kyakotsmovi (1965)

E3695 A handled red bowl (or basket effigy) is decorated with black stylized bird designs by Nettie Ami at Sichomovi (1968)

E5780 A Plainware whistle is designed as a prairie dog effigy by Claudie Fredericks at Kyakotsmovi (1972)

E5491a–c Plainware snail effigies by Eugene Fredericks at Kyakotsmovi (1971)

E6130 A black on red chicken effigy is fashioned from a bowl by Beth Sakeva at Tewa (1973)

E8529 A black on red turtle effigy (1960–1970)

E8575 Black geometric design on a yellow Christmas ornament, by Cynthia Komalestewa at Polacca (1981)

CATALOG

Determining specific use for the objects in the collection would be at best arbitrary. Standardized catalog terminology, therefore, was retained for the catalog entries; for the photo captions a more general terminology was adopted. For example, a stew bowl in the catalog is referred to as a serving bowl in the caption; the catalog lists a piki bowl, whereas the caption may refer to the object as a mixing bowl.

Standarded pottery terminology has been used for the descriptions in the catalog: b = black (color ranges from dark brown to almost true black); r = red; y = yellow (color ranges from peach to yellow to orange); w = white (color ranges from white to buff to yellow). B&r/y = black and red designs painted onto a yellow vessel.

An asterisk (*) indicates those items that are identified with a maker's hallmark. The use of a hallmark has not been as widely used by Hopi potters as it is used by Hopi silversmiths. It is more common for a potter to paint her signature on the vessel, along with her village.

Catalog Number	Object Name	Maker	Date of Manufacture	Location
1178/L	Plainware jar	unknown	1800s	
1550/L	Plainware jar	unknown	1800–1900	
2417-45/L	B&r/y jar	unknown	1920	
2417-46/L	B&w/r jar	unknown	1920	
2417-48/L	B&w/r jar	unknown	1920	
2417-49/L	B&w/r jar	unknown	1920	
2417-50/L	B&w/r jar	unknown	1920	
OC12	Canteen	unknown	1900–1920	
OC21a	B&r/y jar	unknown	1880–1920	
OC71	Ladle	unknown	1800–1840	
OC72	B&r/y bowl	unknown	1900–1920	
OC73	Stew bowl	unknown	1890–1920	
OC74	Ladle	unknown	1800–1850	
OC75	Plainware jar	unknown	1850–1900	
OC76	Ladle	unknown	1800–1850	
OC156	B&r/y bowl	unknown	1900	
OC214	B/y jar	unknown	1900–1930	
OC215	B&r/y jar	unknown	1880–1930	
OC217	Ladle	unknown	1800–1840	
OC218	Scoop	unknown	1840–1865	
OC219	Ladle	unknown	1800–1850	
OC220	B&r/y bowl	unknown	1840–1880	
OC221	B/y bowl	unknown	1840–1880	
OC222	B&r/y jar	unknown	1880–1930	
OC223	B&r/y bowl	unknown	1800–1840	
OC224	B&r/y bowl	unknown	1800–1840	
OC225	B&r/y bowl	unknown	1800–1840	
OC240	Effigy	unknown	1850–1928	
OC241	Stew bowl	unknown	1890–1928	
OC313	Plainware jar	unknown	1800s	
OC400	Unfired jar	Kate Seeni	1931	Walpi
OC439	B/y jar	unknown	1880–1900	
OC470	B/y jar	unknown	1895–1920	
OC482a	B&r/y bowl	unknown	1870–1900	
OC483	Stew bowl	unknown	1880–1900	
OC484	B&r/y bowl	unknown	1900–1950	
OC485	B&r/y jar	unknown	1870–1900	
OC486	B/r jar	unknown	1920–1930	
OC516	Canteen	unknown	1900–1920	
OC517	B&r/y bowl	unknown	1850–1900	
OC994	Stew bowl	unknown	1850–1870	
OC995	Stew bowl	unknown	1900–1930	
OC996	Stew bowl	unknown	1900–1930	
OC997	Stew bowl	unknown	1900–1930	
OC998	Stew bowl	unknown	1840–1870	
OC999	Stew bowl	unknown	1840–1870	
OC1000	Stew bowl	unknown	1900–1930	
OC1001	B&r/y bowl	unknown	1830–1880	
OC1002	Stew bowl	unknown	1870–1910	
OC1003	B&r/y bowl	unknown	1860–1880	
OC1004	Stew bowl	unknown	1870–1900	
OC1005	Stew bowl	unknown	1860–1880	

Catalog Number	Object Name	Maker	Date of Manufacture	Location
OC1006	Stew bowl	unknown	1860–1900	
OC1007	Piki bowl	unknown	1890–1910	
OC1008	Stew bowl	Nawisumy	1923	Oraibi
OC1010	B&r/y bowl	unknown	1900–1950	
OC1011	Piki bowl	Nuvangeumuma	1897	Shungopovi
OC1012	B&r/y bowl	unknown	1800s	
OC1013	Stew bowl	unknown	ca. 1900	
OC1014	Stew bowl	unknown	1870–1900	
OC1015	Stew bowl	Tyvewynka	1895	Shungopovi
OC1016	B/y bowl	unknown	1850–1900	
OC1017	B/y bowl	unknown	1890–1910	
OC1018	Stew bowl	unknown	1880–1910	
OC1019	Stew bowl	unknown	1820–1880	
OC1020	Stew bowl	unknown	1800–1850	
OC1021	Plainware jar	unknown	1850–1900	
OC1022	B&r/y bowl	unknown	1830–1870	
OC1023	B&r/y bowl	unknown	1900s	
OC1024	Stew bowl	unknown	1830–1870	
OC1025	Ladle	unknown	pre-1820	
OC1026	Stew bowl	unknown	1800–1850	
OC1027	B&r/y jar	unknown	1890	
OC1028	B&r/y bowl	unknown	1830–1870	
OC1029	Plainware jar	unknown	1900	
OC1031	Plainware bowl	unknown	1850–1900	
OC1032	Stew bowl	unknown	1870–1900	
OC1033	Stew bowl	unknown	1870–1900	
OC1034	B&r/y bowl	unknown	1850–1900	
OC1035	Stew bowl	unknown	1880–1910	
OC1036	B&r/y bowl	unknown	1800–1840	
OC1037	B&r/y bowl	unknown	1890–1910	
OC1038	Piki bowl	unknown	1885–1915	
OC1039	B&r/y bowl	unknown	1830–1870	
OC1040	B/y bowl	unknown	1900–1930	
OC1041	Ladle	unknown	1800–1830	
OC1042	B&r/y jar	unknown	1870–1900	
OC1044	Stew bowl	unknown	1860–1880	
OC1045	B&r/y bowl	unknown	1890s	
OC1046	Stew bowl	unknown	1870–1900	
OC1047	Scoop	unknown	1800–1830	
OC1048	Ladle	Rose	1900–1928	Shungopovi
OC1049	Stew bowl	unknown	1870–1900	
OC1050	Piki bowl	unknown	1870–1900	
OC1051	Canteen	unknown	1890	
OC1052	B/y jar	unknown	1900–1930	
OC1053	B/y jar	unknown	1900–1930	
OC1054	B&r/y jar	unknown	1870–1900	
OC1055	B&r/y jar	unknown	1870–1900	
OC1056	Piki bowl	Nawisumy	1926	Oraibi
OC1057	B&r/y bowl	unknown	1870–1880	
OC1058	B&r/y jar	unknown	1900	
OC1059	B&r/y jar	unknown	1890–1920	
OC1060	Stew bowl	unknown	1850–1900	

Catalog Number	Object Name	Maker	Date of Manufacture	Location
OC1060a	B&r/y jar	unknown	1890–1920	
OC1061	Plainware jar	Tyvewynka	1892–1895	Shungopovi
OC1062	Piki bowl	unknown	1870–1900	
OC1063	Stew bowl	unknown	1860–1880	
OC1064	B&r/y bowl	unknown	1880–1920	
OC1065	Unfired bowl	Nuvangienima	1899	Shungopovi
OC1067	Unfired jar	Nuvangienima	1889	Shungopovi
OC1067a	Unfired jar	Nuvangienima	1900	Shungopovi
OC1068a	Unfired bowl	Nuvangienima	1889	Shungopovi
OC1069	B&r/y jar	unknown	1900–1930	
OC1071	Stew bowl	unknown	1870–1900	
OC1072	Stew bowl	unknown	1800–1850	
OC1073	Stew bowl	unknown	1800–1850	
OC1074	B&r/y jar	unknown	1900–1920	
OC1075	B&r/y jar	unknown	1900–1920	
OC1076	B/y jar	unknown	1880–1900	
OC1077	Piki bowl	unknown	1900	
OC1078	Plainware jar	Qumanquimka	1895	Shungopovi
OC1079	Plainware jar	Tyvewynka	1887–1890	Shungopovi
OC1080	Ladle	unknown	1800–1840	
OC1081	Canteen	unknown	1900–1920	
OC1082	Stew bowl	unknown	1840–1870	
OC1083	Piki bowl	Nawisumy	1923	Oraibi
OC1084	Piki bowl	unknown	1885–1915	
OC1085	White jar	Qomahoinimam's grandmother	1875–1900	Shungopovi
OC1086	Stew bowl	unknown	1860–1880	
OC1087	Stew bowl	unknown	1880–1920	
OC1088	Piki bowl	Qomanquiamka	1897	Shungopovi
OC1089	Piki bowl	unknown	1870–1900	
OC1090	Plainware jar	Hunimimka	1850–1910	Hotevilla
OC1091	Piki bowl	Emma's grandmother	1885–1915	Oraibi
OC1092	Plainware jar	Hunimimka	1928	Hotevilla
OC1093	Yellow jar	unknown	1700–1800	
OC1094	Plainware jar	unknown	1890–1929	
OC1095	Plainware jar	unknown	1905	
OC1096	Canteen	Hunimimka	1908–1910	Hotevilla
OC1097	Red jar	unknown	1880–1920	
OC1099	Red jar	unknown	1855–1870	
OC1100	Plainware jar	grandmother of Daisy Goshquapinima	1880	Oraibi
OC1101	Plainware jar	unknown	1928	
OC1102	Plainware jar	grandmother of Daisy Goshquapinima	1880	Oraibi
OC1103	Plainware jar	Hunimimka	1923	Hotevilla
OC1104	Plainware jar	unknown	1880	
OC1105	Stew bowl	unknown	1860–1880	
OC1107	Plainware bowl	Hunimimka	1908	Hotevilla
OC1108	Redware bowl	Mabel Tcosytiwa's mother	1928	Hotevilla
OC1109	Scoop	Susie's mother	1900–1910	Oraibi
OC1110	B/y jar	unknown	1928	Hotevilla
OC1112	Ladle	unknown	1920–1950	
OC1113	Miniature jar	unknown	1928	Shungopovi

Catalog Number	Object Name	Maker	Date of Manufacture	Location
OC1114	Plainware jar	Tyvewynka	1875–1880	Shungopovi
OC1115	B/y jar	unknown	1880–1900	
OC1146	Miniature jar	unknown	1900–1920	
OC1149	Plainware jar	Talashoynum	1855	Oraibi
OC1150	Plainware jar	Talashoynum	1854	Oraibi
OC1151	Plainware jar	unknown	1880	Oraibi
OC1152	Plainware jar	Ross's mother	1830–1850	Oraibi
OC1153	Plainware jar	King's mother-in-law	1860	Oraibi
OC1154	Plainware jar	unknown	1880	
OC1155	Plainware jar	Nawisoi	1926	Oraibi
OC1156	Plainware jar	unknown	1880	
OC1159	Plainware bowl	Susie's grandmother	1880	Oraibi
OC1470b	B&r/y bowl	unknown	1880–1920	
OC1472	B/y jar	unknown	1880–1910	
OC1699b	Canteen	unknown	1900–1930	
OC1706b	Plainware jar	unknown	1930	
OC1821	B&r/y jar	unknown	1840–1880	
OC1823	Miniature jar	unknown	1900–1930	
OC1824	Miniature jar	unknown	1900–1930	
OC1829	Plainware jar	unknown	pre-1929	
OC1830	Plainware jar	unknown	pre-1929	
OC1839	Stew bowl	unknown	1920–1930	
OC1840	B&r/y bowl	unknown	1900–1930	
OC1847	Plainware jar	unknown	1700–1800	
OC2166	B&r/y jar	unknown	1880–1900	
OC2383	Ladle	unknown	1700–1800	
OC2734j	Piki bowl	unknown	1930	
OC2735b	Unfired bowl	Poolisie	1940–1950	Sichomovi
OC2735c	Unfired jar	Poolisie	1940–1950	Sichomovi
OC2735e	Unfired jar	Poolisie	1940–1950	Sichomovi
OC2735h	Unfired jar	Poolisie	1940–1950	Sichomovi
OC2735m	Unfired jar	Poolisie	1940–1950	Sichomovi
OC2735n	B&r/y jar	Poolisie	1930s	Sichomovi
OC2735p	B/y bowl	unknown	1925–1930	
OC2780	Plainware jar	Quoiyanginima	1931	Sichomovi
OC2781	B&r/y jar	Sadie Adams	1930	Tewa Village
OC2782	B/y jar	Grace Chapella	1930s	Tewa Village
OC2783	Canteen	Cash Longka	1930	Hotevilla
OC2784	B/r bowl	unknown	1930	
E9a	Stew bowl	unknown	1870–1900	
E16	B&r/y bowl	unknown	1850s	
E18	B/y bowl	Leona Polacca	1900–1930	Tewa Village
E25a	Tile	unknown	1897	
E25b	Tile	unknown	1897	
E25c	Tile	unknown	1897	
E25d	Tile	unknown	1897	
E25e	Tile	unknown	1897	
E25f	Tile	unknown	1897	
E25g	Tile	unknown	1897	
E25h	Tile	unknown	1897	
E25i	Tile	unknown	1897	
E25j	Tile	unknown	1897	

Catalog Number	Object Name	Maker	Date of Manufacture	Location
E25k	Tile	unknown	1897	
E29	Unfired bowl	Brooks	1930–1940	
E30	Unfired jar	unknown	1900–1930	
E32	Ladle	unknown	1850–1900	
E34	Plainware bowl	unknown	1890–1910	
E35	Yellow jar	unknown	1800s	
E36	Plainware jar	unknown	1800s	
E37	Yellow jar	unknown	1800s	
E38	B&r/y jar	unknown	1800s	
E39	Misc. form: Effigy	unknown	1500	
E71	B&r/y jar	unknown	1900–1935	
E73	B&r/y jar	unknown	1880–1930	
E74	B&r/y jar	unknown	1900	
E75	B&r/y jar	unknown	1900–1930	
E76	B&r/y jar	Nampeyo	1900–1930	Tewa Village
E77	B&r/y jar	unknown	1900–1930	
E78	B/y jar	unknown	1900–1930	
E79	B/y jar	unknown	1900–1930	
E80	Red jar	unknown	1900–1925	
E94	Miniature jar	Polevanka	1920–1935	Sichomovi
E95	Miniature jar	Polevanka	1920–1935	Sichomovi
E149	Canteen	unknown	1931	Hotevilla
E154	Plainware jar	unknown	1850–1900	
E155	Plainware jar (pitched)	Cyashongka	1935	Hotevilla
E156	B/y jar	Nampeyo	1912	Tewa Village
E157	B&r/y bowl	Susie Bacon	1935	Sichomovi
E158	Plainware jar	Quoiyanginima	1934	Sichomovi
E183	Piki bowl	unknown	1931	
E184	Piki bowl	unknown	1931	
E185	Misc. form: ash tray	unknown	1933	
E186	White jar	unknown	1931	Oraibi
E187	B/r bowl	Theresa Harvey	1931	Walpi
E188a	Tile	Sadie Adams	1933	Tewa Village
E188b	Tile	Sadie Adams	1933	Tewa Village
E189	B/y jar	unknown	1933	
E190	Ladle	unknown	1931	
E191	Miniature jar	Annie Nampeyo (Mrs. Willie Healing)	1925–1936	Tewa Village
E193	B/y jar	unknown	1932	
E194	Plainware jar	Quoiyanginima	1931	Sichomovi
E195	Misc. form: double lobed	unknown	1900–1936	
E196	B&r/y bowl	unknown	1931	
E197	Plainware jar	Kochahonawe	1935	Walpi
E198	B/r jar	unknown	1934	
E199	B/r bowl	Tewanginema	1933	Sichomovi
E200a	Plainware bowl	Mrs. Sequoptewa	1936	Hotevilla
E200b	Plainware bowl	Mrs. Sequoptewa	1936	Hotevilla
E200c	Plainware bowl	Mrs. Sequoptewa	1936	Hotevilla
E200d,e,f	Ladles (3)	Mrs. Sequoptewa	1933	Hotevilla
E204	Miniature canteen	unknown	1930–1936	
E214	Red jar	Polivenka	1900	Sichomovi
E215	B&r/y bowl	Nampeyo	1920s	Tewa Village

Catalog Number	Object Name	Maker	Date of Manufacture	Location
E233a–c	B/r bowls (3)	Poolisie	1937	Sichomovi
E245	B&r/y jar	Fannie Polacca Nampeyo	1936	Polacca
E304	Misc. form: double jar	Tewanginema	1937	Sichomovi
E305	Plainware jar	Quoiyanginima	1937	Sichomovi
E363	Plainware jar	Tewavensi	1938	Hotevilla
E368	Ladle	unknown	1750–1825	
E369	B&r/y jar	unknown	1900–1930	
E370	B&w/r jar	unknown	1923	
E371	B&r/y jar	unknown	1923	
E372	B/y bowl	unknown	1901	
E380	B&r/w jar	unknown	1800–1850	
E381	B/y jar	unknown	1750–1800	
E383	B/y jar	unknown	1923	
E387	B&r/y jar	unknown	1913	
E388	Bowl	unknown	1905	
E389	B/r bowl	unknown	1923	Walpi
E391	B/y jar	unknown	1800–1870	
E392	B&r/y bowl	unknown	1923	Walpi
E393	B/y bowl	unknown	1850–1900	
E398	B&w/r jar	unknown	1905–1923	
E409	Plainware jar	unknown	1923	Oraibi
E410	B/y jar	unknown	1920–1923	Shungopovi
E411	B&r/y jar	unknown	1885–1900	
E413	B/r bowl	Poolisie	1938	Sichomovi
E414	Stew bowl	Audrey Honi	1938	Tewa Village
E426	Tile	Sadie Adams	1936	Tewa Village
E427	B&r/y bowl	Tewanginema	1938	Sichomovi
E428	Piki bowl	Charlotte Pala	1931	Tewa Village
E429	Piki bowl	Polevanka	1934	Sichomovi
E431	B&r/y jar	Sadie Adams*	1936	Tewa Village
E432	Piki bowl	Poolisie	1934	Sichomovi
E433	B&r/y jar	Fanny Polacca Nampeyo	1922	Tewa Village
E434	B&r/y jar	Siayowsi	1922	First Mesa
E435	B&r/y jar	unknown	1922	
E436	Stew bowl	unknown	1900–1930	
E437	B&r/y jar	Laura Timothy	1936	Tewa Village
E438	B&r/y jar	unknown	1930s	
E439	Stew bowl	Ella Tiwa	1935	Sichomovi
E440	B&r/y jar	Mrs. Keely	1930–1940	Tewa Village
E441	Plainware bowl	unknown	1880–1920	
E442	White jar	Lucy Cochise	1931	Sichomovi
E443	Plainware jar	Kate Seeni	1930	Walpi
E444	Unfired bowl	Poolisie	1938	Sichomovi
E445	Unfired ladle	Poolisie	1938	Sichomovi
E446	Unfired jar	Poolisie	1938	Sichomovi
E447	Plainware jar	unknown	1930s	
E449	Ladle	Younga	1931	Walpi
E450	B/y jar	Tewanginema	1938	Sichomovi
E451	Plainware jar	Kate Seeni	1931	Walpi
E452	Piki bowl	Mabel Dashee	1938	Walpi
E453	Piki bowl	Myrtle Luke Young	1938	Tewa Village
E454	Piki bowl	Poolisie	1938	Sichomovi

Catalog Number	Object Name	Maker	Date of Manufacture	Location
E455	Yellow jar	Lenmana Namoki	1932	Walpi
E456	Yellow jar	Tewavensi	1932	Hotevilla
E457	Canteen	unknown	1930s	Hotevilla
E458	B/y jar	unknown	1925–1935	Walpi
E459	B&w/r jar	Kochahonawe	1936	Walpi
E460	B&r/y jar	unknown	1930s	
E461	Stew bowl	Fay Tray-wa	1930	Tewa Village
E464	B&r/y jar	unknown	1920s	
E465	B/y bowl	unknown	1910–1930	
E466	B&r/y jar	Leona Polacca	1900–1930	Tewa Village
E467	B&w/r jar	unknown	1938	
E468	B&r/y bowl	unknown	1938	
E469	B&r/y bowl	Siayowsi	1938	Tewa Village
E470	B&r/y bowl	unknown	1922	
E477	B/y jar	unknown	1922	
E478	Plainware jar	unknown	1935	
E481	Canteen	Tewavensi	1935	Hotevilla
E483	Canteen	Tewavensi	1935	Hotevilla
E484	Canteen	Tewavensi	1933	Hotevilla
E487	Stew bowl	unknown	1800–1850	
E489	B&r/y jar	unknown	1910–1930	
E496	B&r/y jar	Chorosie	1937	Tewa Village
E498	Canteen	unknown	1938	Hotevilla
E507	Canteen	unknown	1939	
E515	B&r/y jar	Mrs. Solo	1939	Tewa Village
E516	B&r/y bowl	Sadie Adams*	1939	Tewa Village
E517	Ladle	Emma Tagsmana	1939	Walpi
E518	B&r/y jar	Irene Gilbert Shupla*	1938	Tewa Village
E519	B&r/y jar	Kate Seeni	1939	Walpi
E521	B&r/y bowl	Joy Navasie*	1939	Tewa Village
E522	B/y jar	Tewanginema	1939	Sichomovi
E523	B/r jar	Paqua Naha*	1939	Tewa Village
E526	Canteen	unknown	1900–1920	
E527	B&r/y jar	unknown	1905	
E553	B/y bowl	Tewanginema	1939	Sichomovi
E555	Piki bowl	Siwirinepnina	1939	Hotevilla
E556	Piki bowl	Myrtle Luke (Young)	1939	Tewa Village
E558	White jar	Quioyanginima	1939	Sichomovi
E559	Plainware jar	Sinimpka	1939	Hotevilla
E610	Piki bowl	Potsung	1940	Tewa Village
E611	B&r/y jar	Betty Harvey	1940	Tewa Village
E612	B&r/y jar	Matilda Williams	1940	Sichomovi
E613	B&r/y jar	Virginia Cheunsey Naha*	1940	Tewa Village
E614	Canteen	Lena Charlie*	1940	Tewa Village
E615	B&r/y bowl	Fannie Polacca Nampeyo	1930–1940	Tewa Village
E652	Piki bowl	Poolisie	1941	Sichomovi
E699	Plainware jar	Sinimpka	1942	Hotevilla
E700	B&r/y jar	Fannie Polacca Nampeyo	1930	Tewa Village
E709	B/y bowl	unknown	1870–1910	
E710	B/y bowl	unknown	1890–1920	
E711	B/y bowl	unknown	1890–1920	
E712	Stew bowl	unknown	1870–1900	

Catalog Number	Object Name	Maker	Date of Manufacture	Location
E714	Yellow jar	unknown	1800s	
E770	B/y jar	Nampeyo	1900–1921	Tewa Village
E798	B&r/y bowl	unknown	1920–1940	
E799	Tile	unknown	1890–1900	
E800	Tile	unknown	1890–1900	
E801	Tile	unknown	1890–1900	
E802	Tile	unknown	1890–1900	
E803	Tile	unknown	1890–1900	
E804	Tile	unknown	1890–1900	
E805	Tile	unknown	1890–1900	
E806	Tile	unknown	1890–1900	
E807	Tile	unknown	1890–1900	
E808	Tile	unknown	1890–1900	
E809	Tile	unknown	1890–1900	
E810	Tile	unknown	1890–1900	
E811	Tile	unknown	1890–1900	
E812	Tile	unknown	1890–1900	
E813	Tile	unknown	1890–1900	
E814	Tile	unknown	1890–1900	
E815	Tile	unknown	1890–1900	
E816	Tile	unknown	1890–1900	
E817	Tile	unknown	1890–1900	
E818	Tile	unknown	1890–1900	
E819	Tile	unknown	1890–1900	
E820	Tile	unknown	1890–1900	
E821	Tile	unknown	1890–1900	
E822	Tile	unknown	1890–1900	
E823	Tile	unknown	1890–1900	
E824	Tile	unknown	1890–1900	
E825	Tile	unknown	1890–1900	
E826	Tile	unknown	1890–1900	
E827	Tile	unknown	1890–1900	
E828	Tile	unknown	1890–1900	
E829	Tile	unknown	1890–1900	
E830	Tile	unknown	1890–1900	
E831	Tile	unknown	1890–1900	
E832	Tile	unknown	1890–1900	
E833	Tile	unknown	1890–1900	
E834	Tile	unknown	1890–1900	
E835	Tile	unknown	1890–1900	
E836	Tile	unknown	1890–1900	
E837	Tile	unknown	1890–1900	
E847a,b	Ladles	Poolisie	1941	Sichomovi
E849	B&r/y jar	unknown	1918	
E852	B&w/r jar	unknown	1900–1915	
E853	B&r/y jar	unknown	1918	
E854	Yellow jar	unknown	1918	
E855	B&w/r jar	Nampeyo (attr)	1918	Tewa Village
E857	Stew bowl	unknown	1840–1880	
E858	B&r/y jar	unknown	1918	
E859	B&r/y jar	unknown	1870–1900	
E908	B&r/y jar	unknown	1900–1940	

Catalog Number	Object Name	Maker	Date of Manufacture	Location
E947	B&r/y bowl	Fannie Polacca Nampeyo	1940–1952	Tewa Village
E972	B/r jar	Kate Seeni	1948	Walpi
E982	B/y bowl	unknown	1930s	
E1002	B/r jar	Viola Howto	1950	Sichomovi
E1003	B&r/y bowl	Mildred Youvella	1950	Tewa Village
E1004	Plainware jar	Rebecca Sulu	1950	Tewa Village
E1029	B&r/y jar	Rachel Nampeyo	1951	Polacca
E1072	Plainware bowl	Alice James	1952	Oraibi
E1095	Plainware jar	Peheuminima	1953	Hotevilla
E1107	Plainware bowl	unknown	unknown	
E1108	Plainware bowl	unknown	1850–1920	
E1109	Plainware jar (black)	unknown	1900–1953	
E1110	Plainware jar	unknown	1890–1920	
E1111	Plainware jar	unknown	1900–1953	
E1114	Yellow jar	unknown	1900–1953	
E1115	Yellow jar	unknown	1900–1953	
E1116	Plainware jar	unknown	1900–1930	
E1117	Plainware jar	unknown	1900–1953	
E1118	Plainware jar	unknown	1900–1953	
E1119	Plainware jar	unknown	1900–1953	
E1122	Piki bowl	unknown	1930–1953	
E1123	Plainware bowl	unknown	1890–1910	unknown
E1140	Unfired jar	unknown	1930–1954	
E1153	Plainware jar	unknown	1900–1954	Hotevilla
E1154	B/y bowl	unknown	1890–1910	
E1225	Plainware jar	Peheuminima	1940	Hotevilla
E1226	Plainware jar	Peheuminima	1940	Hotevilla
E1227	Plainware jar	Peheuminima	1940	Hotevilla
E1228	Plainware jar	unknown	1900–1930	
E1229	Plainware jar (black)	unknown	1900–1930	
E1230	Plainware jar	unknown	1900–1930	
E1231	Plainware jar	unknown	1900–1930	
E1247	Misc. form: wind chime	Rachel Nampeyo	1940–1950	Tewa Village
E1250	Ladle	Vera Nevahoioma Pooyouma	1954	Hotevilla
E1260	Stew bowl	unknown	1890–1920	
E1261	Stew bowl	unknown	1870–1900	
E1262	B&r/y bowl	unknown	1800s	
E1263	B/y jar	unknown	1810–1850	
E1264	Canteen	unknown	1600s	
E1265	Canteen	unknown	1910	Oraibi
E1266	B&r/y bowl	unknown	1890–1920	
E1294	B/r bowl	unknown	1930–1940	
E1296	Yellow jar	unknown	1900–1956	
E1297	Canteen	unknown	1890–1920	
E1298	Misc. form: shoe	Treva James Burton	1954	Oraibi
E1299	Plainware bowl	Treva James Burton	1954	Oraibi
E1300	Plainware bowl	Treva James Burton	1954	Oraibi
E1301	Canteen	unknown	1800s	
E1302	Canteen	unknown	1800s	
E1303	Canteen	unknown	1800s	Oraibi
E1304	Plainware jar	unknown	1850–1900	
E1305	Plainware bowl	owned by Tewaquaptewa's grandmother	1850–1900	Oraibi

Catalog Number	Object Name	Maker	Date of Manufacture	Location
E1310	Canteen	unknown	1956	Oraibi
E1311	B&w/r bowl	Faye Avatchoya	1956	Tewa Village
E1312	Redware bowl	Flora Ray	1956	Tewa Village
E1315	B/r jar	Garnet Pavatea	1956	Tewa Village
E1316	B/r bowl	Garnet Pavatea	1956	Tewa Village
E1317	B&r/y jar	unknown	1890–1920	
E1318	Plainware bowl	unknown	1930–1960	Hotevilla
E1379	Plainware jar	unknown	1940s	
E1404	B/r bowl	unknown	1920–1950	
E1407	Tile	Sadie Adams	1930–1945	Tewa Village
E1408	Tile	Sadie Adams	1930–1945	Tewa Village
E1409	Tile	Sadie Adams*	1930–1945	Tewa Village
E1410	Tile	Annie Nampeyo	1930–1950	Tewa Village
E1411	B&r/y jar	Nampeyo and Fannie Polacca Nampeyo	1934	Tewa Village
E1412	B&w/r bowl	Tewanginema	1900–1933	Sichomovi
E1413	B&r/y bowl	Myrtle Luke Young	1930–1957	Tewa Village
E1414	Piki bowl	Tewanginema	1933	Sichomovi
E1415	Plainware jar	Quoiyanginima	1934	Sichomovi
E1417	B&r/y jar	Annie Nampeyo (Mrs. Willie Healing)	1950	Tewa Village
E1418	B&r/y jar	Audry Honi	1945–1955	Tewa Village
E1419	B&r/y jar	Paqua Naha*	1935	Tewa Village
E1448a–e	Tile (5)	unknown	1930	
E1453	Redware bowl	unknown	1957	
E1465	B&w/r jar	Garnet Pavatea	1958	Tewa Village
E1466	B&w/r bowl	Garnet Pavatea	1958	Tewa Village
E1467	Red cookie jar	Sadie Adams	1958	Hano
E1468	Plainware bowl	Ada Fredericks	1958	Kyakotsmovi
E1469	Plainware bowl	Ada Fredericks	1958	Kyakotsmovi
E1476	B&r/y jar	Marcia Fritz	1958	Sichomovi
E1482	B&r/y jar	unknown	1700–1730	
E1495	B&r/y jar	unknown	1920–1928	
E1496	B/y jar	unknown	1923	
E1503	B/r jar	Garnet Pavatea	1959	Tewa Village
E1505	Plainware bowl	Elizabeth White	1959	Kyakotsmovi
E1516	Plainware jar	unknown	1930s	
E1519	Plainware jar	Hannah K.	1900–1930	Shungopovi
E1913	Canteen	unknown	1930–1960	
E1915	Tile	Laura Tamosie	1964	Tewa Village
E1916	Tile	Laura Tamosie	1964	Tewa Village
E1917	Tile	Laura Tamosie	1964	Tewa Village
E1919	Tile	Laura Tamosie	1964	Tewa Village
E1920	Tile	Laura Tamosie	1964	Tewa Village
E1921	Tile	Laura Tamosie	1964	Tewa Village
E1922	B/y bowl	Alice James	1964	Oraibi
E1923	Plainware jar	Louise Nahsongya	1964	Sichomovi
E1933	Tile	Sadie Adams	1933–1943	Hano
E1937	Ladle	Bessie Monongya	1964	Oraibi
E1942	B&r/y jar	unknown	1850–1875	
E1968	Tile	unknown	1890–1900	
E1969	Tile	unknown	1890–1900	
E1970	Tile	unknown	1890–1900	

Catalog Number	Object Name	Maker	Date of Manufacture	Location
E1971	Tile	unknown	1890–1900	
E1972	Unfired bowl	unknown	1954	
E1973	Unfired bowl	unknown	1954	
E1974	Unfired jar	unknown	1954	
E1975	Unfired bowl	unknown	1954	
E1976	Unfired bowl	unknown	1954	
E1977	Unfired bowl	unknown	1954	
E1979	Unfired bowl	unknown	1954	
E1980	Unfired pitcher	unknown	1954	
E1981	Unfired bowl	unknown	1954	
E1982	Unfired pitcher	unknown	1954	
E1983	Unfired ladle	unknown	1954	
E1993	B&r/y jar	unknown	1910–1928	
E1994	B&r/y jar	unknown	1910–1923	
E1995	B&r/y jar	unknown	1910–1923	
E1996	B&r/y bowl	unknown	1900–1923	
E2006	B&r/y bowl	unknown	1910–1920	
E2009	White jar	unknown	1900–1930	
E2016	Plainware jar	Emogene Lomakema	1960s	Walpi
E2206	Plainware bowl	Alice Sakiestewa	1960	Kyakotsmovi
E2207	B&r/y jar	Lena Charlie*	1960	Tewa Village
E2208	B/r jar	Garnet Pavatea	1960	Tewa Village
E2209	Plainware bowl	Nellie Toopkema	1930–1960	Bacabi
E2219	B/y bowl	Garnet Pavatea	1961	Tewa Village
E2220	B&r/y bowl	Alice Seabiyestewa	1961	Kyakotsmovi
E2221	Redware bowl	Sadie Adams*	1961	Tewa Village
E2241	Canteen	Norma Ami	1961	Sichomovi
E2243	B&r/y bowl	unknown	1925–1930	
E2244	Misc. form: effigy pitcher	unknown	1930	
E2348	Canteen	unknown	1900	
E2349	Canteen	unknown	1900	
E2350	Plainware jar	unknown	1900–1960	
E2365	B/y bowl	unknown	1880–1900	
E2366	B/y jar	unknown	1900–1920	
E2422	B/y bowl	unknown	1900s	
E2485a–d	Plainware bowls (4)	Barbara Fredericks	1962	Kyakotsmovi
E2485e	Plainware bowl	Barbara Fredericks	1962	Kyakotsmovi
E2486b	Plainware bowl	unknown	1950–1962	
E2488	Ladle	Lorraine Shula	1962	Walpi
E2491a,b	Misc. form: cup (2)	unknown	1930–1960	
E2493	Tile	Laura Tamosie	1962	Tewa Village
E2505	B&r/y bowl	unknown	1960–1970	
E2578	Misc. form: napkin ring	unknown	1930–1960	
E2580	Stew bowl	unknown	1870–1900	
E2582	Tile	Sadie Adams*	1930	Tewa Village
E2583	Tile	Sadie Adams*	1930	Tewa Village
E2585	B&r/y jar	unknown	1930	
E2586	Piki bowl	unknown	1930	
E2587	B&r/y jar	unknown	1930s	
E2589	Piki bowl	unknown	1930–1963	
E2590	Tile	Sadie Adams	1930	Tewa Village
E2591	Tile	Sadie Adams	1930	Tewa Village

Catalog Number	Object Name	Maker	Date of Manufacture	Location
E2593	Tile	unknown	1930	
E2602	B&r/y bowl	unknown	1942	
E2603	Misc. form: bowl	unknown	1942	
E2604	Misc. form: bowl	unknown	1942	
E2605	Misc. form: ashtray	unknown	1942	
E2606	Piki bowl	unknown	1930–1963	
E2621	Plainware bowl	unknown	1930–1963	
E2622	Misc. form: pig	unknown	1963	
E2630	B&r/y jar	Nampeyo and Fannie Polacca Nampeyo	1935	Polacca
E2634	B&r/y bowl	Nampeyo	1911	Tewa Village
E2638a,b	Redware jar	Violet Huma	1963	Sichomovi
E2639a,b	White jar	Bessie Monongya	1963	Oraibi
E2640	B&r/y bowl	Viola Howto	1963	Sichomovi
E2641	Stew bowl	Rena Kavena	1963	Sichomovi
E2642	B&r/y bowl	Laura Tamosie	1963	Tewa Village
E2856	Stew bowl	unknown	1870–1900	
E2940	B&r/y jar	Poolisie	1935	Sichomovi
E2941	B&r/y jar	Paqua Naha*	1931–1953	Tewa Village
E2942	Canteen	unknown	1930	Hotevilla
E2943	B&r/y jar	Poolisie	1933	Sichomovi
E2944	Piki bowl	Charlotte Pala	1930	Tewa Village
E2994	Plainware bowl	Bessie Monongya	1962	Oraibi
E2995	Tile	Sadie Adams*	1955	Tewa Village
E3005	Canteen	unknown	1910–1920	
E3006	B/y bowl	unknown	1870–1900	
E3007	Ladle	unknown	1870–1910	
E3017	Misc. form: wind chime	Elizabeth White	1965	Kyakotsmovi
E3056	Yellow jar	unknown	1850–1900	
E3057	Plainware jar	unknown	1900	
E3058	Plainware jar	unknown	1900	
E3123	Plainware jar	Bessie Monongya	1965	Oraibi
E3124	Tile	Carol Namoki	1965	Tewa Village
E3135	B&r/y bowl	unknown	1940–1960	
E3178	B&r/y bowl	unknown	1930–1940	
E3179	Misc. form: B/b jar	Helen Naha*	1964	Polacca
E3180	Black jar	Edna Sequi	1964	Polacca
E3283	Bowl	unknown	1890	
E3304	Ladle	unknown	1800–1860	
E3311	B/r & b/w bowl	Marsha Fritz	1966	Sichomovi
E3312	B&r/y bowl	Rena Kavena	1966	Sichomovi
E3313	Redware bowl	Nancy Lewis	1966	Sichomovi
E3314	Redware jar	Clara Peesha	1966	Sichomovi
E3315	Plainware jar	Vera Pooyouma	1966	Hotevilla
E3316	Yellow jar	Nettie Ami	1966	Sichomovi
E3317	Wedding jar	Helen Naha*	1966	Tewa Village
E3318	B/r bowl	Ethel Youvella	1966	Tewa Village
E3319	Plainware bowl	Ada Fredericks (Dawamana)	1966	Kyakotsmovi
E3374	B&r/y bowl	unknown	1940	
E3375	B&w/r bowl	unknown	1940	
E3376	B/y bowl	unknown	1940	
E3432	White jar	unknown	1930s	

Catalog Number	Object Name	Maker	Date of Manufacture	Location
E3433	Misc. form: canteen bank	unknown	1940s	
E3434	Plainware jar	Nasimosi	1880–1900	Oraibi
E3445	Black jar	unknown	1880–1920	
E3447	B&r/y jar	Daisy Nampeyo	1950	Polacca
E3456	B/y bowl	Helen Naha*	1967	Tewa Village
E3457	B&r/y jar	Laura Tamosie	1967	Tewa Village
E3458	B/y bowl	Rosie Talasie	1967	Sichomovi
E3508	Misc. form: artificial potsherd	Garnet Pavatea	1967	Tewa Village
E3521	Plainware jar	unknown	1880–1920	
E3522	B&r/y-o-w bowl	Fannie Polacca Nampeyo	1930–1940	
E3542	B/r jar	Sadie Adams	1967	Tewa Village
E3543	B/r jar	Sadie Adams*	1967	Tewa Village
E3665	B/y bowl	unknown	1930–1940	
E3694	B/r & b/w bowl	Emogene Lomakema	1968	Polacca
E3695	B/r bowl	Nettie Ami	1968	Sichomovi
E3696	B&r/y bowl	Laura Tamosie	1968	Tewa Village
E3697	B&r/y bowl	Patty Maho	1968	Tewa Village
E3698	B/r bowl	Carol Namoki	1968	Tewa Village
E3849	Redware bowl	Garnet Pavatea	1968	Tewa Village
E3850	Ladle	Garnet Pavatea	1968	Tewa Village
E3852	Misc. form: turtle	Eugene Fredericks	1968	Kyakotsmovi
E3853a,b	Misc. form: turtle	Carolyn Talyemtewa	1968	Polacca
E3854	Plainware jar	Bessie Monongya	1968	Oraibi
E3892	Misc. form: bell clapper	Barbara Fredericks (Pahongsi)	1968	Kyakotsmovi
E3906	Plainware jar	unknown	1900s	
E4079	Miniature canteen	unknown	1930–1970	
E4139	Plainware bowl	unknown	1700	
E4157	B&r/y jar	Emogene Lomakema	1969	Walpi
E4158	Ladle	Laura Tamosie	1969	Tewa Village
E4159	Misc. form: effigy bowl	(Marian) Sulu Tewaginema	1969	Sichomovi
E4160	Misc. form: cup	Bessie Monongya	1969	Oraibi
E4161	Ladle	Vera Pooyouma	1969	Hotevilla
E4162	Misc. form: wind chime	Idelle George	1969	Oraibi
E4163	Misc. form: wind chime	Elizabeth White	1969	Kyakotsmovi
E4164	Tile	Laura Tamosie	1969	Tewa Village
E4165	B&r/y jar	Theresa Harvey	1969	Walpi
E4166	White jar	Elizabeth White	1969	Kyakotsmovi
E4203	B&r/y bowl	unknown	1800–1870	
E4204	B&r/y bowl	unknown	1800–1870	
E4205	B&r/y bowl	unknown	1800–1870	
E4206	B&r/y bowl	unknown	1800–1870	
E4212	B/r & b/w bowl	Carol Namoki	1969	Tewa Village
E4224a	Redware bowl	Garnet Pavatea	1968	Tewa Village
E4224b	Ladle	Garnet Pavatea	1968	Tewa Village
E4437	B&r/y jar	unknown	1890–1920	Oraibi
E4438	B&r/y jar	unknown	1890–1920	
E4439	B&r/y bowl	unknown	1880–1900	
E4440	Scoop	unknown	1900–1920	
E4441	Miniature canteen	unknown	1900–1940	Oraibi
E4442	B/r bowl	unknown	1900–1920	
E4443	B&r/y bowl	unknown	1880–1890	

Catalog Number	Object Name	Maker	Date of Manufacture	Location
E4444	B/y bowl	unknown	1890–1920	
E4446	B&r/y bowl	unknown	1900	
E5045	B&r/y bowl	unknown	1850–1870	
E5046	B&r/y bowl	unknown	1850–1880	
E5048a,b,c	Miniature anthropomorphic figurines (3)	Elizabeth White	1969	Kyakotsmovi
E5093	Miniature canteen	Charlotte Silas	1970	Hotevilla
E5094	B&r/y	Bertha Kinalie	1970	Walpi
E5095	Miniature jar	Garnet Pavatea	1970	Tewa Village
E5096	Ladle	Lucy Nahee	1970	Sichomovi
E5097	Miniature dog	Claude Fredericks	1970	Kyakotsmovi
E5099	Miniature bowl	Laura Tamosie	1970	Tewa Village
E5100	Misc. form: wind chime	Elizabeth White	1970	Kyakotsmovi
E5112a,b	Miniature animals	Vivian Shula	1970	Tewa Village
E5125	B/y bowl	unknown	1900–1950	
E5219	Stew bowl	unknown	1880–1920	
E5220	Stew bowl	unknown	1900–1930	
E5221	Stew bowl	unknown	1920	
E5222	B/y bowl	unknown	1880–1900	
E5223	B&r/y bowl	Ella Tiwa	1954	Sichomovi
E5224	B&r/y bowl	Emma Heyah	1930–1950	Walpi
E5225	B&r/y bowl	Garnet Pavatea	1954	Tewa Village
E5226	Ladle	Rachel Cuya	1954	Walpi
E5227	B&r/y bowl	Ella Tiwa	1954	Sichomovi
E5228	B&r/y bowl	Ella Tiwa	1954	Sichomovi
E5229	Miniature jar	Wilma Rose Pavatea	1957	Tewa Village
E5230	Miniature bowl	Rachel Nampeyo	1960–1970	Polacca
E5231	Miniature bowl	Fannie Polacca Nampeyo	1940–1950	Polacca
E5233	Canteen	unknown	pre-1900	
E5234	Canteen	Elizabeth White	1961	Kyakotsmovi
E5352	B/y jar	Fannie Polacca Nampeyo	1950	Polacca
E5353	B&r/y jar	unknown	1930–1940	
E5368	Ladle	Rosetta Huma	1974	Sichomovi
E5369	Plainware jar	Sekayumka	1800–1850	Moencopi
E5370	B&r/y jar	Lorna Lomakema	1974	Tewa Village
E5381	Tile	unknown	1918	
E5382	Tile	unknown	1918	
E5383	Tile	unknown	1918	
E5384	Tile	unknown	1918	
E5385	Tile	unknown	1918	
E5386	Tile	unknown	1918	
E5387	Tile	unknown	1918	
E5388	Tile	unknown	1918	
E5389	Tile	unknown	1918	
E5390	Tile	unknown	1918	
E5391	Tile	unknown	1918	
E5392	Tile	unknown	1918	
E5393	Tile	unknown	1918	
E5394	Tile	unknown	1918	
E5395	Tile	unknown	1918	
E5396	Tile	unknown	1918	
E5397	Tile	unknown	1918	

Catalog Number	Object Name	Maker	Date of Manufacture	Location
E5398	Tile	unknown	1918	
E5399	Tile	unknown	1918	
E5400	Tile	unknown	1918	
E5403	B&r/y bowl	Flora Ray	1936	Tewa Village
E5404	B/y bowl	Flora Ray	1936	Tewa Village
E5405	B&r/y jar	Flora Ray	1936	Tewa Village
E5406	Scoop	Flora Ray	1936	Tewa Village
E5408	B/y bowl	Poolisie	1937	Sichomovi
E5411	B/y bowl	Poolisie	1937	Sichomovi
E5412	B/y bowl	Poolisie	1937	Sichomovi
E5413	B/y bowl	Poolisie	1940	Sichomovi
E5414	B/y bowl	Poolisie	1940	Sichomovi
E5415	B/y bowl	Poolisie	1940	Sichomovi
E5416	Unfired bowl	Poolisie	1938	Sichomovi
E5417	B&r/y bowl	Poolisie	1941	Sichomovi
E5418	B/y bowl	Poolisie	1941	Sichomovi
E5419	B/y bowl	Kate Seeni	1955	Walpi
E5420	B/y jar	unknown	1940	
E5445	Plainware jar	unknown	1930s	
E5446	Plainware jar	unknown	1930s	
E5449	Stew bowl	unknown	1840–1880	
E5450	Stew bowl	unknown	1900–1920	
E5451	B/r bowl	unknown	1900–1930	
E5452	Plainware bowl	unknown	1900	
E5470	Plainware bowl	Vera Pooyouma	1971	Hotevilla
E5484	Misc. form: rattle	Eleanor Ami	1971	Tewa Village
E5491a–c	Misc. form: effigy (3)	Eugene Fredericks	1971	Kyakotsmovi
E5746	Red jar	unknown	1930s	
E5748	B&r/y bowl	Elva Nampeyo	1962–1972	Polacca
E5749	B&r/y jar	Fannie Polacca Nampeyo	1962–1972	Polacca
E5750	B&r/y jar	Leah Nampeyo	1962–1972	Polacca
E5751	B&r/y jar	Fannie Polacca Nampeyo	1962–1972	Polacca
E5752	B&r/y jar	Fannie Polacca Nampeyo	1962–1972	Polacca
E5753	B&r/y jar	Fannie Polacca Nampeyo	1962–1972	Polacca
E5758	Redware bowl	Faye Avatchoya	1957	Tewa Village
E5759	Piki bowl	Emma Adams	1957	Sichomovi
E5773a,b	B&r/y jar	Emogene Lomakema	1972	Walpi
E5778	B&r/y bowl	Patricia Honie	1972	Sichomovi
E5780	Misc. form: whistle	Claudie Fredericks	1972	Kyakotsmovi
E5788	Plainware jar	Alice James	1972	Oraibi
E5897	Redware jar	Bessie Monongya	1972	Oraibi
E5898a,b	B&r/y jar	Nettie Ami	1972	Sichomovi
E5932	Plainware bowl	unknown	1900–1910	
E5934	Plainware jar (black)	unknown	1880–1900	
E5963	Wedding jar	Carol Namoki	1973	Tewa Village
E5964	B/r bowl	Ella Mae Talashie	1973	Walpi
E5965	B/r jar	Verna Nahee	1972	Sichomovi
E6130	B/r bowl	Beth Sakeva	1973	Tewa Village
E6142	B&r/y bowl	unknown	1625–1725	
E6196a,b	Misc. form: teapot and lid	Marion Sulu	1973	Sichomovi
E6197a,b	Misc. form: cup and saucer	Marion Sulu	1973	Sichomovi
E6199	Canteen	Vera Pooyouma	1973	Hotevilla

Catalog Number	Object Name	Maker	Date of Manufacture	Location
E6206	Piki bowl	Violet Huma	1973	Sichomovi
E6247	Misc. form: bowl	Alice James	1973	Oraibi
E6248	B/y jar	Bessie Monongya	1973	Oraibi
E6259	B/r jar	Treva Burton	1973	Oraibi
E6290	Scoop	unknown	1950–1965	
E6306	Misc. form: effigy	Patricia Honie	1973	Polacca
E6307a,b	B&r/y jar and lid	Anita Polacca	1973	Polacca
E6308a,b	Misc. form: fork and spoon	Zella Cheeda	1973	Sichomovi
E6309a–f	Redware bowls (6)	Zella Cheeda*	1973	Sichomovi
E6311	Piki bowl	Myrtle Luke Young	1973	Tewa Village
E6332	B&r/y bowl	unknown	1930	
E6350	Ladle	unknown		
E6351	Miniature jar	Rachel Nampeyo	1973	Polacca
E6352	B&r/y jar	Tonita Hamilton Nampeyo	1973	Polacca
E6353a,b	B/y jar	Eleanor Lucas (Nampeyo)	1973	Gallup, N.M.
E6354	B&r/y jar	Fannie Polacca Nampeyo	1973	Polacca
E6355	B&r/y jar	Nellie Nampeyo Douma	1973	Polacca
E6356	B&r/y jar	Priscilla Namingha Nampeyo	1973	Polacca
E6359	B&r/y jar	Nellie Nampeyo	1973	Polacca
E6360	B&r/y bowl	Betsy Nampeyo Koopee	1973	Polacca
E6361	B&r/y jar	Rachel Nampeyo	1973	Polacca
E6363	B&r/y jar	Dextra Qüotskuyva Nampeyo	1973	Polacca
E6364	Redware bowl	Dextra Qüotskuyva Nampeyo	1973	Polacca
E6365	B/y jar	Camille Qüotskuyva Nampeyo*	1973	Polacca
E6366	B&r/y jar	Marie Nampeyo Koopee	1973	Polacca
E6387	Plainware jar	Vera Pooyouma	1973	Hotevilla
E6581	B&r/y bowl	unknown	1880–1920	
E6582	B&r/y jar	unknown	1900–1920	
E6583	B&w/r bowl	unknown	1920–1950	
E6584	B&w/r bowl	Paqua	1920–1950	Tewa Village
E6585	B/y jar	unknown	1920	
E6609	Tile	unknown	1900–1930	
E6610	Tile	unknown	1930–1960	
E6611	Tile	unknown	1930–1960	
E6612	Tile	unknown	1930–1960	
E6613	Tile	unknown	1930–1960	
E6614	Tile	unknown	1930–1960	
E6615	Tile	unknown	1930–1960	
E6616	Tile	unknown	1930–1960	
E6617	Tile	unknown	1930–1960	
E6618	Tile	unknown	1930–1960	
E6619	Tile	unknown	1930–1960	
E6620	Tile	unknown	1930–1960	
E6621	Tile	unknown	1930–1960	
E6622	Tile	unknown	1930–1960	
E6623	Tile	unknown	1940–1960	
E6624	Tile	unknown	1940–1960	
E6625	Tile	unknown	1940–1960	
E6626	Tile	unknown	1940–1960	
E6627	Tile	unknown	1940–1960	
E6628	Tile	unknown	1940–1960	
E6629	Tile	unknown	1940–1960	

Catalog Number	Object Name	Maker	Date of Manufacture	Location
E6630	Tile	unknown	1940–1960	
E6631	Tile	unknown	1940–1960	
E6632	Tile	unknown	1940–1960	
E6639	B&r/y jar	unknown	1940–1960	
E6640	B&r/y jar	unknown	1940–1960	
E6642	B/y jar	unknown	1900–1930	
E6643	B/y jar	unknown	1924	Hotevilla
E6644	Miniature canteen	unknown	1940–1960	
E6645	Misc. form: ashtray	unknown	1940–1960	
E6646	Misc. form: jar	unknown	1940–1960	
E6647	Ladle	unknown	1930–1960	
E6648	Ladle	unknown	1930–1960	
E6649	Ladle	unknown	1930–1960	
E6650	Misc. form: match holder	unknown	1940–1960	
E6651	Misc. form: effigy	unknown	1940–1960	
E6652	B&r/y bowl	unknown	1940–1960	
E6653	B&r/y jar	unknown	1940–1960	
E6654	B&r/y jar	unknown	1940–1960	
E6655	B&r/y jar	unknown	1940–1960	
E6656	B/y jar	unknown	1940–1960	
E6657	B/y jar	unknown	1940–1960	
E6658	B/y jar	unknown	1940–1960	
E6659	B/y bowl	unknown	1940–1960	
E6660	Misc. form: effigy	unknown	1940–1960	
E6661	Ladle	unknown	1850–1900	
E6662	B&r/y bowl	unknown	1940–1960	
E6663	B/y bowl	unknown	1940–1960	
E6664	B/y bowl	unknown	1940–1960	
E6665	B/y bowl	unknown	1940–1960	
E6666	B&r/y bowl	unknown	1940–1960	
E6667	Canteen	unknown	1940–1960	
E6668	B&r/y bowl	unknown	1940–1960	
E6669	B&r/y bowl	unknown	1940–1960	
E6670	B/y bowl	unknown	1940–1960	
E6671	B/y bowl	unknown	1940–1960	
E6672	Miniature canteen	unknown	1940–1960	
E6673	B&r/y jar	unknown	1940–1960	
E6674	Stew bowl	unknown	1900–1920	
E6675	B/y jar	unknown	1924	
E6676	B/y jar	unknown	1940–1960	
E6677	B/y jar	unknown	1940–1960	
E6678	Misc. form: ashtray	unknown	1940–1960	
E6679	Misc. form: cylinder	unknown	1940–1960	
E6680	B/r jar	unknown	1920–1974	
E6681	B/y bowl	unknown	1940–1960	
E6682	B/y jar	unknown	1974	
E6765	B&r/y bowl	unknown	1890–1900	
E6766	B&r/y jar	unknown	1940–1960	
E6775	Plainware bowl	unknown	1940–1960	
E6777	Misc. form: plate	unknown	1940–1960	
E6781	Plainware bowl	unknown	1940–1960	
E6783	Red jar	unknown	1940–1960	

Catalog Number	Object Name	Maker	Date of Manufacture	Location
E6916	Canteen	unknown	unknown	
E6925a,b	Misc. form: barrettes (2)	John Poleahla	1974	Sichomovi
E6957	B/r bowl	unknown	1966	
E6982	B&r/y bowl	Paqua or Joy Navasie*	1950s	Tewa Village
E7122	Stew bowl	unknown	1870–1900	
E7123	Stew bowl	unknown	1870–1900	
E7124a,b,c	Stew bowl	unknown	1860–1890	
E7125a,b	Stew bowl	unknown	1840–1880	
E7126a,b	Stew bowl	unknown	1870–1900	
E7127a,b,c	Stew bowl	unknown	1840–1890	
E7196	Miniature canteen	unknown	1971	
E7201	Canteen	unknown	1900s	
E7205	Miniature jar	unknown	1800–1900	
E7206	Miniature jar	unknown	1800–1900	
E7207	Miniature jar	unknown	1800–1900	
E7210	Misc. form: bowl	Zella Cheeda	1975	Sichomovi
E7211	Ladle	Nettie Ami	1975	Sichomovi
E7234	B&r/y jar	unknown	1880s	
E7368	Stew bowl	unknown	1850–1920	
E7380	B&r/y jar	unknown	1890–1900	
E7381	B&r/y jar	unknown	1900	
E7412	Miniature bowl	unknown	1930–1960	
E7413	Miniature bowl	unknown	1930–1960	
E7423a	Redware bowl	Vivian Mumzewa	1976	Sichomovi
E7423b–e	Ladles (4)	Vivian Mumzewa	1976	Sichomovi
E7424	B/y bowl	Hattie Navajo	1976	Sichomovi
E7437	B&r/y jar	Sadie Adams*	1930–1970	Tewa Village
E7443	Miniature ladle	unknown	1930–1970	
E7444	B&r/y bowl	unknown	1920–1950	
E7447	B&r/y jar	unknown	1930–1970	
E7448	B&r/y jar	unknown	1930–1970	
E7452	B&r/y bowl	unknown	1940–1960	
E7454	B&w/r bowl	Faye Avatchoya	1930–1950	
E7471	Plainware jar	unknown	1970	
E7472	Misc. form: wind chime	Elizabeth White	1968–1969	Kyakotsmovi
E7476	Plainware jar	unknown	1950–1900	
E7560	Miniature canteen	unknown	1900–1915	
E7561	B&r/y bowl	unknown	1850–1900	
E7563	Canteen	unknown	1880–1915	
E7564	B&r/y bowl	unknown	1900–1915	
E7565	B&r/y bowl	unknown	1900–1915	
E7566	B/y bowl	unknown	1880–1900	
E7567	Canteen	unknown	1900–1915	
E7568	B/y bowl	unknown	1900–1915	
E7569	B/y bowl	unknown	1900–1915	
E7570	B&r/y jar	Nampeyo(?)	1890–1915	Tewa Village
E7571	B/y jar	Nampeyo (attr)	1900–1915	Tewa Village
E7572	B&w/r jar	Nampeyo (attr)	1904–1915	Tewa Village
E7573	B&w/r jar	Nampeyo (attr)	1900–1915	Tewa Village
E7606	R/y bowl	Vera Pooyouma	1976	Hotevilla
E7610	B/r bowl	Hattie Nampeyo	1977	Sichomovi
E7629	Tile	unknown	1910–1930	

Catalog Number	Object Name	Maker	Date of Manufacture	Location
E7630	Tile	unknown	1910–1930	
E7631	Tile	unknown	1910–1930	
E7632	Tile	unknown	1910–1930	
E7633	Tile	unknown	1910–1930	
E7634	Tile	unknown	1910–1930	
E7635	Tile	unknown	1910–1930	
E7636	Tile	unknown	1910–1930	
E7637	Tile	unknown	1910–1930	
E7638	Tile	unknown	1910–1930	
E7639	Tile	unknown	1910–1930	
E7640	Tile	unknown	1900–1930	
E7641	Tile	unknown	1910–1930	
E7642	Tile	unknown	1910–1930	
E7643	Tile	unknown	1910–1930	
E7644	Tile	unknown	1910–1930	
E7645	Tile	unknown	1910–1930	
E7646	Tile	unknown	1910–1930	
E7647	Tile	unknown	1910–1930	
E7648	Tile	unknown	1910–1930	
E7649	Tile	unknown	1910–1930	
E7650	Tile	unknown	1910–1930	
E7651	Tile	unknown	1910–1930	
E7652	Tile	unknown	1910–1930	
E7653	Tile	unknown	1910–1930	
E7654	Tile	unknown	1910–1930	
E7656	B&w/r jar	unknown	1910–1930	
E7658	B/y jar	unknown	post-1930	
E7659	B&r/y jar	Nellie Nampeyo	1910–1930	Polacca
E7660	Stew bowl	unknown	1885–1920	
E7661	B&r/y jar	Nellie Nampeyo	1910–1930	Polacca
E7662	B&r/y jar	unknown	1900–1910	
E7663	Miniature canteen	unknown	1910–1930	
E7664	B&r/y jar	Nampeyo	1910–1930	Tewa Village
E7665	B&r/y bowl	unknown	1910–1930	
E7666	B&w/r jar	Nampeyo	1910–1930	Tewa Village
E7667	B/y bowl	unknown	1910–1930	
E7669	B&r/y jar	unknown	1910–1930	
E7672	Miniature bowl	Rachel Nampeyo	1910–1930	Polacca
E7673	B&w/r bowl	unknown	1910–1930	
E7674	B/y bowl	unknown	1910–1930	
E7675	B&r/y bowl	unknown	1910–1930	
E7676	B/y bowl	unknown	1910–1930	
E7678	B&r/y jar	Nampeyo	1900–1930	Tewa Village
E7679	B&r/y jar	Nampeyo	1910–1930	Tewa Village
E7680	B&r/y jar	unknown	1910–1930	
E7681	Redware bowl	unknown	1910–1930	
E7682	B&r/y jar	Daisy Nampeyo	1910–1930	Polacca
E7683	B&r/y jar	Nampeyo	1910–1930	Tewa Village
E7740	B&r/y bowl	unknown	1890–1920	
E7741	B&r/y bowl	unknown	1930–1960	
E7742	Misc. form: bowl/jar	unknown	1890–1920	
E7755	Misc. form: turtle	unknown	1950–1965	

Catalog Number	Object Name	Maker	Date of Manufacture	Location
E7756	Misc. form: turtle	unknown	1950–1965	
E7790	Ladle	unknown	1600s	
E7802	B/r jar	Evelyn Poolheco	1977	Walpi
E7803	Miniature canteen	Irma Tewasva	1977	Sichomovi
E7804	Wedding jar	Nancy Lewis	1977	Sichomovi
E7858	Ladle	unknown	1700s	
E7863	B&r/y jar	Sadie Adams*	1930–1940	Tewa Village
E7864	B&r/y jar	Sadie Adams*	1930–1940	Tewa Village
E7871	Wedding jar	Nancy Lewis	1971	Sichomovi
E7872	Canteen	Eleanor Ami	1977	Tewa Village
E7873	Redware bowl	Laura Tamosie	1970	Tewa Village
E7874	B/y jar	Clarice Sahmi	1977	Sichomovi
E7875	Redware bowl	unknown	1965–1975	
E7876	Misc. form: cup	unknown	1950–1965	
E7877	B/y bowl	unknown	1800s	
E7878	Ladle	Pahongsi (Barbara Fredericks)	1968	Kyakotsmovi
E7879	Miniature jar	unknown	1930–1970	
E7881	Ladle	Garnet Pavatea	1969	Tewa Village
E7882	Ladle	Garnet Pavatea	1960	Tewa Village
E7884	Redware lid	unknown	1955–1970	
E7885	B&w/r bowl	Garnet Pavatea	1977	Tewa Village
E7915	B&r/y jar	Elava Nampeyo	1969	Polacca
E7918	B&r/y jar	Leah Nampeyo	1969	Polacca
E8007	Misc. form: ashtray	unknown	1930–1950	
E8008a,b	B&r/y jar and lid	Laura Tamosie	1959–1961	Tewa Village
E8009	Red jar	Rena Kavena	1961	Sichomovi
E8010	Stew bowl	Garnet Pavatea	1950	Tewa Village
E8039	B&r/y bowl	Priscilla Namingha Nampeyo	1977	Tewa Village
E8042	Miniature bowl	unknown	1970–1977	
E8154	Miniature jar	Vera Pooyouma	1978	Hotevilla
E8163	B&r/y jar	Claudina Lomakema	1978	Polacca
E8210	Miniature bowl	Dextra Qüotskuyva Nampeyo	1972	Polacca
E8283	B&r/y bowl	unknown	1900–1940	
E8289	Misc. form: lampshade	unknown	1940–1960	
E8300	Canteen	Simaonim	1885–1900	Oraibi
E8377	B&r/y jar	Jean Youvella Nampeyo	1979	Polacca
E8384	Miniature jar	Clara Peesha	1979	Sichomovi
E8387	Ladle	Rena Kavena	1979	Sichomovi
E8388	Ladle	Annie Nampeyo (Juanita Healing)	1979	Tewa Village
E8398	Redware jar	Al Qöyawayma	1978	Scottsdale, Ariz.
E8422	Plainware bowl	Elizabeth White	1979	Kyakotsmovi
E8423	Stew bowl	Rena Kavena	1977	Sichomovi
E8424	Piki bowl	Garnet Pavatea	1978	Tewa Village
E8529	Misc. form: Turtle Effigy	unknown	1960–1970	
E8540	Stew bowl	unknown	1890–1910	
E8558	B/r bowl	Rena Kavena	1965–1975	Sichomovi
E8559	Redware bowl	Patty Maho	1969	Tewa Village
E8560	B&r/w jar	Nancy Lewis	1979	Sichomovi
E8561	Misc. form: effigy bowl	Flora Ray	1940–1960	Tewa Village
E8562	B/y bowl	Norma Ami	1950–1960	Sichomovi
E8563	Tile	Sadie Adams*	1930–1935	Tewa Village

Catalog Number	Object Name	Maker	Date of Manufacture	Location
E8564	Tile	Sadie Adams*	1930–1935	Tewa Village
E8565	Tile	Sadie Adams*	1930–1935	Tewa Village
E8566	Tile	Sadie Adams*	1930–1935	Tewa Village
E8567	Tile	Sadie Adams*	1930–1935	Tewa Village
E8568	Tile	Sadie Adams*	1930–1935	Tewa Village
E8569	Tile	Sadie Adams*	1930–1935	Tewa Village
E8570	Tile	Sadie Adams*	1930–1935	Tewa Village
E8571a,b	Misc. form: mortar & pestle	Vera Pooyouma	1981	Hotevilla
E8572	Ladle	Vera Pooyouma	1981	Hotevilla
E8573	Miniature canteen	Alice James	1981	Oraibi
E8574	Miniature seed jar	Dextra Qüotskuyva Nampeyo	1981	Polacca
E8575	Misc. form: Christmas ornament	Cynthia Komalestewa	1981	Polacca
E8591	White bowl	Elizabeth White	ca. 1966	Kyakotsmovi
E8599	Stew bowl	Marcella Kahe	1982	Sichomovi
E8664	B/r bowl	Geneva Pavatea	1969	Tewa Village
E8665	Piki bowl	Nancy Lewis	1969	Sichomovi
E8666	B&r/y jar	Theresa Harvey	1974	Walpi
E8667	Ladle	Vera Pooyouma	1977	Hotevilla
E8668	Redware jar lid	unknown	1960–1980	
E8741	Ladle	unknown	1950–1960	
E8742	B&w/r bowl	unknown	1950–1960	
E8744	Stew bowl	unknown	1950–1960	
E8745	Scoop	unknown	1950–1960	
E8747	B/y bowl	unknown	1950–1960	
E8756	Wedding jar	Helen Naha*	1983	Tewa Village
E8757	B&r/w jar	Natalie Navasie*	1983	Tewa Village
E8765	B/r jar	Nannie Talahongva	1980	Tewa Village
E8788	B&r/y jar	Ethel Youvella	1972	Tewa Village
E8791	Stew bowl	Garnet Pavatea	1981	Tewa Village
E8792	Redware bowl	Garnet Pavatea	1981	Tewa Village
E8793	Redware bowl	Garnet Pavatea	1980–1981	Tewa Village
E8796	B&r/y jar	Paqua Naha	1930–1950	Tewa Village
E8797	B/y bowl	unknown	1950–1960	
E8798	B&r/y jar	unknown	1950–1960	

Designed by Pamela Scott Lungé
Type: Trump
Typography by Tiger Typographics
Text Paper: Centura Dull Book
Cover: Kromekote
Photographs by Horizons West
Printed by Classic Printers

HALLMARKS

Sadie Adams

Lena Charlie

Zella Cheeda

Lorna Lomakema

Bessie Monongya

Paqua Naha

Virginia Cheunsey Naha

Helen Naha

Daisy Nampeyo

Dextra Qüotskuyva
Nampeyo

Fannie Nampeyo

Tonita Nampeyo

Joy Navasie

Natalie Navasie

Irene Gilbert
Shupla

BIBLIOGRAPHY

ADAMS, E. CHARLES. 1979. Walpi Archaeological Project: Phase II. Volume 3. Native Ceramics. A report submitted to Heritage Conservation and Recreation Service, Interagency Archeological Service, San Francisco. A partial fulfillment of the Requirement of Contract No. C2504. Copies on file at Museum of Northern Arizona, Flagstaff, Arizona.

ALLEN, LAURA GRAVES. 1980–1984. Author's field journals.

APPLEGATE, FRANK to F. H. DOUGLAS. Letter dated 12/12/30. Manuscript No. 207-306-2. Museum of Northern Arizona, Flagstaff, Arizona.

BARTLETT, KATHARINE. 1977. "A History of Hopi Pottery in Hopi and Hopi-Tewa Pottery." *Plateau* Vol. 49, No. 3. Museum of Northern Arizona, Flagstaff, Arizona.

BUNZEL, RUTH. 1972. *The Pueblo Potter: A Study of Comparative Imagination in Primitive Art.* Dover reprint of 1929 Columbia University Press.

COLTON, HAROLD SELLERS. 1939. "The Hopi Craftsman Celebrates Its Tenth Birthday." *1939 Hopi Craftsman Exhibition.* Museum of Northern Arizona, Flagstaff, Arizona.

———. 1949. *Hopi Kachina Dolls with a Guide to Their Identification.* University of New Mexico, Albuquerque, New Mexico.

———. 1953. Potsherds, An Introduction to the Study of Prehistoric Southwestern Ceramics. *Bulletin* No. 25, Museum of Northern Arizona, Flagstaff, Arizona.

———. 1954. Checklist of Southwestern Pottery Types. Museum of Northern Arizona *Ceramic Series* No. 2.

COLTON, HAROLD S. and LYNDON LANE HARGRAVE. 1937. Handbook of Northern Arizona Pottery Wares. Museum of Northern Arizona *Bulletin* No. 11, Flagstaff, Arizona.

COLTON, MARY-RUSSELL FERRELL. 1930a. Report to the Board of Trustees. May 8, 1930. On file at Museum of Northern Arizona, Flagstaff, Arizona.

———. 1930b. *1930 Hopi Craftsman Exhibition.* Museum of Northern Arizona, Flagstaff, Arizona.

———. 1931. Field Instructions. 1931 Hopi Craftsman Exhibition. Museum of Northern Arizona, Flagstaff, Arizona.

———. 1932. Guidelines. 1932 Hopi Craftsman Exhibition. Museum of Northern Arizona, Flagstaff, Arizona.

———. 1933. Letter to National Association of Indian Affairs. On file (MS. 207-306-1) Museum of Northern Arizona, Flagstaff, Arizona.

———. 1937. "Ancient Arts of Hopi Indians Shown at Museum in Arizona." *Christian Science Monitor.* Copy on File 1937 Hopi Craftsman Exhbition. Museum of Northern Arizona, Flagstaff, Arizona.

———. 1965. *Hopi Dyes.* Museum of Northern Arizona Press, Flagstaff, Arizona.

FEWKES, JESSE WALTER. 1973. *Designs on Prehistoric Pottery.* Dover Publications, Inc., New York.

LOVE, SUZANN. 1973. Hopi Tiles. University of Denver Master Thesis.

NEQUATEWA, EDMUND. 1942. "Nampeyo, Famous Hopi Potter 1859?–1942." *Plateau* Vol. 15, No. 1, Museum of Northern Arizona, Flagstaff, Arizona.

SCHMEDDING, JOSEPH. 1951. *Cowboy and Indian Trader.* Caxton Printers, Caldwell, Idaho.

SHEPARD, ANNA O. 1956. *Ceramics for the Archaeologist.* Carnegie Institution, Washington, D.C.

SIKORSKI, KATHRYN A. 1968. *Modern Hopi Pottery.* Monograph Series Vol. XV, No. 2. Utah State University, Logan, Utah.

SMITH, WATSON. 1971. *Painted Ceramics of the Western Mound at Awatovi.* Peabody Museum. Cambridge, Massachusetts.

SMITH, MRS. WHITE MOUNTAIN. 1940. "He is our Friend." *The Desert Magazine,* Vol. 4, No. 1.

———. 1938. "Tom Pavatea, Hopi Trader." *The Desert Magazine,* Vol. 1, No. 4.

STANISLAWSKI, MICHAEL B., BARBARA B. STANISLAWSKI, and ANN HITCHCOCK. 1976. "Identification Marks on Hopi and Hopi-Tewa Pottery." *Plateau* Vol. 48, Numbers 3 and 4. Museum of Northern Arizona, Flagstaff, Arizona.

WADE, EDWIN L. and LEA S. McCHESNEY. 1980. *America's Great Lost Expedition: The Thomas Keam Collection of Hopi Pottery from the Second Hemenway Expedition, 1890–1894.* The Heard Museum, Phoenix, Arizona.

———. 1981. *Historic Hopi Ceramics: The Thomas V. Keam Collection of the Peabody Museum of Archaeology and Ethnology, Harvard University.* Peabody Museum Press.